Engaging God's Word

1&2 Peter

Engage Bible Studies

Tools That Transform

Engage Bible Studies
an imprint of

COMMUNITY BIBLE STUDY

Engaging God's Word: 1 & 2 Peter
Copyright © 2012, 2014 by Community Bible Study. All rights reserved.
ISBN 978-1-62194-004-3

Published by Community Bible Study
790 Stout Road
Colorado Springs, CO 80921-3802
1-800-826-4181
www.communitybiblestudy.org

Printed in the United States of America.

Contents

Introduction

Welcome to the life-changing adventure of engaging with God's Word! Whether this is the first time you've opened a Bible or you've studied the Scriptures all your life, good things are in store for you. Studying the Bible is unlike any other kind of study you have ever done. That's because the Word of God is *"living and active"* (Hebrews 4:12) and transcends time and cultures. The earth and heavens as we know them will one day pass away, but God's Word never will (Mark 13:31). It's as relevant to your life today as it was to the people who wrote it down centuries ago. And the fact that God's Word is living and active means that reading God's Word is always meant to be a personal experience. God's Word is not just dead words on a page—it is page after page of living, powerful words—so get ready, because the time you spend studying the Bible in this *Engaging God's Word* course will be life-transforming!

Why Study the Bible?

Some Christians read the Bible because they know they're supposed to. It's a good thing to do, and God expects it. And all that's true! However, there are many additional reasons to study God's Word. Here are just some of them.

We get to know God through His Word. Our God is a relational God who knows us and wants us to know Him. The Scriptures, which He authored, reveal much about Him: how He thinks and feels, what His purposes are, what He thinks about us, how He views the world He made, what He has planned for the future. The Bible shows us God's many attributes—His kindness, goodness, justice, love, faithfulness, mercy, compassion, creativity, redemption, sovereignty, and so on. As we get to know Him through His Word, we come to love and trust Him.

God speaks to us through His Word. One of the primary ways God speaks to us is through His written Word. Don't be surprised if, as you read the Bible, certain parts nearly jump off the page at you, almost as if they'd been written with you in mind. God is the Author of this incredible book, so that's not just possible, it's likely! Whether it is to find comfort, warning, correction, teaching, or guidance, always approach God's Word with your spiritual ears open (Isaiah 55:3) because God, your loving heavenly Father, has things He wants to say to you.

God's Word brings life. Just about everyone wants to learn the secret to "the good life." And the good news is, that secret is found in God's Word. Don't think of the Bible as a bunch of rules. Viewing it with that mindset is a distortion. God gave us His Word because as our Creator and the Creator of the universe, He alone knows how life was meant to work. He knows that love makes us happier than hate, that generosity brings more joy than greed, and that integrity allows us to rest more peacefully at night than deception does. God's ways are not always "easiest" but they are the way to life. As the Psalmist says, *"If Your law had not been my delight, I would have perished in my affliction. I will never forget Your precepts, for by them You have given me life"* (Psalm 119:92-93).

God's Word offers stability in an unstable world. Truth is an ever-changing negotiable for many people in our culture today. But building your life on constantly changing "truth" is like building your house on shifting sand. God's Word, like God Himself, never changes. What He says was true yesterday, is true today, and will still be true a billion years from now. Jesus said, *"Everyone then who hears these words of Mine and does them will be like a wise man who built his house on the rock"* (Matthew 7:24).

God's Word helps us to pray effectively. When we read God's Word and get to know what He is really like, we understand better how to pray. God answers prayers that are according to His will. We discover His will by reading the Bible. First John 5:14-15 tells us that *"this is the confidence that we have toward Him, that if we ask anything according to His will He hears us. And if we know that He hears us in whatever we ask, we know that we have the requests that we have asked of Him."*

How to Get the Most out of *Engaging God's Word*

Each *Engaging God's Word* study contains key elements that have been carefully designed to help you get the most out of your time in God's Word. Slightly modified for your study-at-home success, this approach is very similar to the tried-and-proven Bible study method that Community Bible Study has used with thousands of men, women, and children across the United States and around the world for nearly 40 years. There are some basic things you can expect to find in each course in this series.

❖ Lesson 1 provides an overview of the Bible book (or books) you will study and questions to help you focus, anticipate, and pray about what you will be learning.

❖ Every lesson contains questions to answer on your own, commentary that reviews and clarifies the passage, and three special sections called "Apply what you have learned," "Think about" and "Personalize this lesson."

❖ Some lessons contain memory verse suggestions.

Whether you plan to use *Engaging God's Word* on your own or with a group, here are some suggestions that will help you enjoy and receive the most benefit from your study.

Spread out each lesson over several days. Your *Engaging God's Word* lessons were designed to take a week to complete. Spreading out your study rather than doing it all at once allows time for the things God is teaching you to sink in and for you to practice applying them.

Pray each time you read God's Word. The Bible is a book unlike any other because God Himself inspired it. The same Spirit who inspired the human authors who wrote it will help you to understand and apply it if you ask Him to. So make it a practice to ask Him to make His Word come alive to you every time you read it.

Read the whole passage covered in the lesson. Before plunging into the questions, take time to read the specific chapter or verses that will be covered in that lesson. Doing this will give you important context for the whole lesson. Reading the Bible in context is an important principle in interpreting it accurately.

Begin learning the memory verse. Learning Scripture by heart requires discipline, but the rewards far outweigh the effort. Memorizing a verse allows you to recall it whenever you need it—for personal encouragement and direction, or to share with someone else. Consider writing the verse on a sticky note or index card that you can post where you will see it often or carry with you to review during the day. Reading and re-reading the verse often—out loud when possible—is a simple way to commit it to memory.

Re-read the passage for each section of questions. Each lesson is divided into sections so that you study one small part of Scripture at a time. Before attempting to answer the questions, review the verses that the questions will cover.

Answer the questions without consulting the Commentary or other reference materials. There is great joy in having the Holy Spirit teach you God's Word on your own, without the help of outside resources. Don't cheat yourself of the delight of discovery by reading the Commentary prematurely. Wait until after you've completed the lesson.

Repeat the process for all the question sections.

Prayerfully consider the "Apply what you have learned," marked with the 📌 push pin symbol. The vision of Community Bible Study is not to just gain knowledge about the Bible, but to be transformed by it. For this reason, each set of questions closes with a section that encourages you to apply what you are learning. Usually this section involves action—something for you to do. As you practice these suggestions, your life will change.

Read the Commentary. *Engaging God's Word* commentaries are written by theologians whose goal is to help you understand the context of what you are studying as it relates to the rest of Scripture, God's character, and what the passage means for your life. Of necessity, the commentaries include the author's interpretations. While interesting and helpful, keep in mind that the Commentary is simply one person's understanding of what these passages mean. Other godly men and women have views that are also worth considering.

Pause to contemplate each "Think about" section, marked with the ☐ notepad symbol. These features, embedded in the Commentary, offer a place to pause and consider some of the principles being brought out by the text. They provide excellent ideas to journal about or to discuss with other believers, especially those doing the study with you.

Jot down insights or prayer points from the "Personalize this lesson" marked with the ☑ check box symbol. While the "Apply what you have learned" section focuses on doing, the "Personalize this lesson" section focuses on becoming. Spiritual transformation is not just about doing right things and refraining from doing wrong things—it is about changing from the inside out. To be transformed means letting God change our hearts so that our attitudes, emotions, desires, reactions, and goals are increasingly like Jesus'. Often this section will discuss something that you cannot do in your own strength—so your response will usually be something to pray about. Remember that becoming more Christ-like is not just a matter of trying harder—it requires God's empowerment.

A Promising Future

When Peter followed Jesus to His trial before the Jewish religious leaders, three times people questioned him about his relationship to His Master. Affirming his relationship to the Lord could have brought him persecution, so each time he was asked, he denied even knowing Jesus. Now, some 30 years after those events—and after the arrival of the promised Holy Spirit—Peter is a different man. Now he's the one advising other believers about how to respond to coming persecution. The Holy Spirit had dramatically changed Peter's life, and now, with persecution approaching and false teachers infiltrating the church, he knew his fellow believers would need that radical change in their lives.

Old Peter	New Peter	Life Lesson
Impatient, skeptical, walked by sight (Matthew 14:28; 16:21-23)	Patient, trusting, walks by faith (1 Peter 1:8-10)	True joy is the product of real faith in the real, risen Lord.
Impetuous, ignorant of Jesus' true identity (Matthew 17:4)	Settled, completely confident in Christ (1 Peter 2:21-24)	Believers can rest assured because of Christ's payment for sin and God's sovereignty.
Misunderstood submission to authority (John 18:10)	Gained a new understanding of authority (1 Peter 2:13-25)	God places people in authority, but all must answer to Him.
(Mistakenly) self-confident (Matthew 26:33-35)	Utterly confident in God and His Word (1 Peter 1:22-24)	Trust in God rather than in self—especially during trials.
Fearful in the face of trials (Matthew 26:69-75)	Understands that trials bring blessings (1 Peter 3:13-17)	Trials are inevitable; God uses them to mold believers and to glorify Himself.

1. Why do you think God chose Peter as a leader for His church?

    _____

    _____

    _____

2. Can you cite an example of trials developing faith and maturity in your life or the life of a friend or relative?

    Divorse) – I have always believed & had faith in God. The lifestyle I chose then was wrong. Found a Born again Christian at a Presbyterian church

3. What connections might there be between Peter's emphasis on growing through trials in his first letter and being wary of false teachers in his second letter?

    _____

    _____

    _____

    _____

If you are doing this study with a group, take time to pray for others in the group who may be facing trials. If you are studying alone, in the space below write a prayer asking God to help you rejoice through the trials that you will face throughout your life.

Lesson 1 Commentary

A Promising Future

Written to believers undergoing trials, hardships, and discouragements, Peter's letters are moving, compassionate responses to human need in light of the gospel of Christ. The believers' persecution is the predictable result of obeying God's authority rather than the ungodly political system under which they live. Their suffering is the means by which their *"faith … may be found to result in praise and glory and honor at the revelation of Jesus Christ"* (1 Peter 1:7). Christ is the perfect model of the righteous Sufferer, who strengthens, encourages, and gives hope to His followers in troubled times.

With Hebrews, James, 1, 2, 3 John, and Jude, Peter's letters form a subdivision of New Testament books called *General Epistles*. Unlike the apostle Paul's letters, originally directed to individual churches, the several authors of the General Epistles all address the church at large and emphasize various points.

Background of 1 Peter

The author of 1 Peter identifies himself as *"Peter, an apostle of Jesus Christ"* (1:1). Although some critics question whether the apostle Peter is the author, strong evidence supports his claim. Frequent references to the example of Christ's suffering indicate the author's familiarity with the Old Testament picture of the Messiah as a Suffering Servant. Parts of the letter bear a striking similarity to Peter's sermons recorded in the book of Acts. Peter also mentions *"Mark, my son"* (5:13), which recalls his affection for that young man and his family (Acts 12:12).

Historical evidence dates the writing in the early AD 60s. The letter is addressed to believers, some of whom were Gentiles *"of the Dispersion in Pontus, Galatia, Cappadocia, Asia and Bithynia"* (1:1). These were

Roman provinces in Asia Minor that are now part of modern Turkey.

Think about the apostle Peter. Some claim 1 Peter is too well written to be authored by a Galilean fisherman. The book of Acts, the record of the early church, notes that Peter was an *"uneducated, common"* man whose courage could be explained only by the fact that he *"had been with Jesus"* (Acts 4:13). Because Peter spent time with Jesus, God used him in unexpected ways. Likewise, as you make time to "be with Jesus" and know Him better, you may be surprised at the way God uses you.

The Letter's Organization

After the author identifies himself and the people to whom he writes, he immediately praises God for the promise of the *"living hope"* (1:3) reserved for believers. This sets a confident, triumphant tone for the remainder of the letter.

The body of 1 Peter is devoted to *exhortation* (meaning *urging, warning,* or *counsel*) in the face of trials. The letter gives three sets of exhortations, each followed by a plea to the readers to look at the example of Christ's sufferings. In 1:13-25, Peter issues a call to God's people based on God's call to *"be holy, for I am holy"* (Leviticus 11:45). The call to holy living is then interpreted from two viewpoints. The first image is that of Israel as a chosen people set apart *from* the nations. The second image pictures Israel scattered or dispersed *among* the nations. The theme of holy living ends by recalling Christ's steadfastness in the face of suffering, *"leaving you an example, so that you might follow in His steps"* (1 Peter 2:21).

A second set of exhortations shifts to household concerns in 3:1-7, with specific advice on Christian marriage. Following these exhortations is the reminder that those who are criticized for their *"good behavior in Christ"* (3:16) should not be surprised or ashamed. The author encourages his readers in their trials by recalling Christ's example of suffering for doing good.

A third set of exhortations begins in chapter 4. Because the end time is near, Peter cautions Christians to live for God by separating themselves from evil and using *"each … gift … to serve one another, as good stewards of God's varied grace"* (4:10). He again reminds believers that they may rejoice in sharing Christ's sufferings because of the reward that awaits them when Christ appears in glory.

The final division of 1 Peter comes in 5:1-11. The author urges church elders to be faithful in their pastoral duties and to follow the example of Jesus. All believers are to stand *"firm in your faith"* (5:9). After a blessing (verses 10-11), Peter mentions Silas, who helped write the epistle. As a biblical symbol of all world systems that oppose God, *"Babylon"* (5:13) may refer here to Rome, where tradition places Peter in his later years.

Key Ideas

This letter rings with confidence in the eventual triumphant outcome of God's purpose for the world. The triumph does not depend on believers, but on the resurrection of Jesus Christ from the dead. This resurrection power, available to all believers, is the key to living a life filled with faith and hope. For raising Jesus from the dead, God deserves complete trust and praise, because *"according to His great mercy, He has caused us to be born again to a living hope"* (1:3).

Believers gain courage in present troubles by looking to the example of Christ in His suffering. The hope for the future Peter speaks of is not wishful thinking, but a future reality secured by Jesus' resurrection. This hope has the power to transform our present lives according to God's will. No other biblical writer seems more eager to draw a connection between faith and behavior. Peter's stress on conduct is not based on principles, but on the person and example of Jesus Christ. Christ redeems believers; Christ upholds and guides believers; and Christ will reward believers. He is both the model and the goal of the redeemed life.

Peter's letter lifts our eyes from present circumstances to the future promise. Christians have been allowed to read the last chapter of history, so to speak, enabling us to "live from the end." In the present, the cross of Christ supplies us with courage; for the future, Christ's resurrection inspires us with confidence and hope.

Personalize this lesson.

✓ God intends for His Word to be a source of encouragement, challenge, and spiritual food. As you allow His Word to penetrate your heart and mind, will you commit yourself to the attitude expressed by the prophet Jeremiah: *"Your words were found, and I ate them, and Your words became to me a joy and the delight of my heart, for I am called by your name, O LORD, God of hosts"* (Jeremiah 15:16).

A Living Hope in Troubling Times
1 Peter 1:1-12

Memorize God's Word: 1 Peter 1:3.

❖ 1 Peter 1:1-12—The Author

1. Read the first 12 verses of Peter's first letter and record your first impressions of

   a. Peter _He loved & believed in the word_
      of the Lord

   b. his mission _To spread the word to all_
      churches
      hope

   c. his message _was our salvation of the_
      soul at the end of the life of our bodies.

2. a. Although the other apostles respected Peter, how does he refer to himself in 1:1 and 5:1?
      Apostle & servant

   b. What does his limited reference to himself suggest about Peter at this stage in his life?
      An Apostle of Jesus.

❖ 1 Peter 1:1-2—Strangers in the World

3. Explain how the phrases Peter uses to describe his original audience are equally true of Christians today.

   God's elect, strangers in the world

4. What roles and activities does <u>Peter attribute</u> to each person of the Trinity?

   a. the Father *God & Father of the Son Jesus.*

   b. the Son *Our Lord*

   c. the Holy Spirit *Sanctifying work of the Spirit.*

5. From Exodus 24:1-8, how would you explain the Old Testament meaning of sprinkling blood? *To be lasting it took written form. Then Moses read for your bills for the blood. Moses then sprinkled on the altar*

There must be shedding of blood for forgiveness.

6. What is the meaning of sprinkling Jesus Christ's blood (Hebrews 9:21-23)? *Jesus on the cross fulfilled the law of the old testament when He died, for all of us before that it was goats & animals.*

7. How is the sprinkling of Jesus' blood different from Old Testament sprinkling (Hebrews 9:22–10:4)? *Jesus' death on the cross took the place of the animals.*

❖ 1 Peter 1:3-9—Living With Hope and Joy

8. What difficult circumstances in his readers' lives does Peter acknowledge?

   Trials to Test our faith. To see if it is strong & pure. More precious to God than Gold.

9. Name at least three things Peter bases his attitudes on as he acknowledges his readers' difficulties (1:3-5).

   Mercy, Born again & hope

10. How would you describe the inheritance Peter emphasizes?

    All honor to God & His boundless mercy

11. From your own experience, what prevents us from displaying the joy of our salvation in our daily lives? (See also Matthew 13:18-23 and Galatians 5:22-23.)

12. From 1 Peter 1:8-9, how would you describe the real meaning of a personal relationship with Jesus Christ?

    My best friend

13. What is distinctive about the faith of the people Peter wrote to—and our faith today (1:8; see also John 20:29; 2 Corinthians 5:7)?

    We believe by faith

❖ 1 Peter 1:10-12—The Gospel

14. What do these verses teach us about how the Old Testament prophets

    a. searched for the gospel message? *Through the Holy Spirit, Christ's suffering dilligent,*

    b. received the gospel message? *Holy Spirit Exiles of the dispersion*

15. a. What was the content of the prophets' message? *The message of Jesus & His suffering grace*

    b. What was the purpose of their message? *The meaning of Christ, in a special way*

16. How do you react when you realize that *"the things that have now been announced to you through those who preached the good news to you by the Holy Spirit sent from heaven, [are] things into which angels long to look"* (1:12)?

    _____

    _____

    _____

Apply what you have learned. There is no greater joy than knowing you are saved. Take some time to praise God for this gift. If you are not sure of your salvation, talk with a pastor, a Bible study leader, or a mature Christian friend.

A Living Hope in Troubling Times
1 Peter 1:1-12

The Greeting

Salutations were an essential part of ancient letters, identifying the author and recipients, and concluding with a greeting. In his salutation, Peter uses few words to list his own credentials: *"Peter, an apostle of Jesus Christ"* (1:1). In the only other place in the letter where he speaks in the first person, Peter calls himself *"a fellow elder and a witness of the sufferings of Christ, as well as a partaker in the glory that is going to be revealed"* (5:1).

More revealing than the letter's destination is its recipients' position. They are *"elect,"* joint heirs of the mighty privileges of Israel in the Old Testament. Peter also calls them *"exiles of the Dispersion."*

As chosen, privileged, and scattered people, believers are also blessed with a threefold relationship with God, *"according to the foreknowledge of God the Father, in the sanctification of the Spirit, for obedience to Jesus Christ and for sprinkling with His blood"* (1:2). Peter identifies each member of the Trinity by an activity:

- ❖ God the Father calls believers according to His sovereign choice and eternal will. The apostle Paul told the Ephesian believers that God *"chose us in Him before the foundation of the world"* and *"predestined us for adoption as sons through Jesus Christ"* (Ephesians 1:4-5). *[handwritten: We were chosen before the world]*

- ❖ God the Holy Spirit does the work of sanctifying believers. The Greek word for *sanctification* means to set apart for service to God. The Holy Spirit equips or outfits believers for *"good works, which God prepared beforehand, that we should walk in them"* (Ephesians 2:10).

- ❖ God the Son sacrificed Himself on our behalf and calls us to obedience. The *"sprinkling with His blood"* (1 Peter 1:2) recalls that at Mount Sinai, Moses sprinkled a blood sacrifice on the altar and on the people as a sign of God's covenant with them. But Israel's animal sacrifices had to be offered repeatedly. Through the blood of Christ, the sinless Lamb of God, sins are forgiven once and for all time (Hebrews 9:25-10:4). Fully divine and fully human, Jesus is the only holy and acceptable sacrifice for human disobedience, and He is our example of perfect obedience to God. Mentioning Him at the beginning of the letter establishes the theme of faithfulness in suffering that will dominate the remainder of Peter's letter.

Living With Hope

Peter ends his salutation with *"grace and peace"* and then begins a hymn of praise to *"the God and Father of our Lord Jesus Christ! According to His great mercy, He has caused us to be born again to a living hope through the resurrection of Jesus Christ from the dead"* (1 Peter 1:3). All three claims—resurrection, new birth, and living hope—are solely God's work. Dead people cannot raise themselves, infants cannot choose to be born, and wishful thinking cannot change the future. But what we cannot do, God has done for us in Christ. Believers are reborn (John 3:3-8). New birth is not the end of the matter, however. Believers are reborn to a living hope, to a new inheritance, and to salvation itself. This present life is not the object of a believer's hope. Our hope is in the Living One, Jesus Christ, who makes *"all things new"* (Revelation 21:5) and for whom all things are possible.

New birth also promises eternal inheritance. In the Old Testament the word *inheritance* refers to the land of Canaan. Since Abraham's time, Israel's hope had focused on Canaan. A Christian's inheritance *"is imperishable, undefiled, and unfading"* (1 Peter 1:4). The inheritance that is *"kept in heaven for you"* is dependent on God's foreknowledge and fatherhood, not on human striving or performance. It rests on *"God's power"* (1:5) and will be revealed according to God's sovereign design *"in the last time."* The inheritance is presently held in trust for believers, who are shielded *"through faith."*

Think about the word *inheritance*. We often consider an inheritance as some *thing*—money or a treasured possession that we will receive in the future. For Christians, the inheritance is not so much some *thing* as it is some *One*. The psalmist sings, *"The LORD is the portion of my inheritance and my cup." "Whom have I in heaven but Thee? And besides Thee, I desire nothing on earth. My flesh and my heart may fail, but God is the strength of my heart and my portion forever"* (Psalm 16:5; Psalm 73:25-26, NASB). If you have been reborn into a living hope, you have the incredible privilege to be an heir of the living God.

Living With Joy

Peter's focus shifts from the future inheritance to present trials: *"In this you rejoice,"* he writes in verse 6. The anchor of their joy sustains believers when they are *"grieved by various trials."* The *"living hope"* of verse 3 is not an escape from trials, but strength in the midst of them. Likewise, joy is found even within trials, not in spite of them.

This knowledge not only assures us that God is present with us in adversity; it spares us from the mistake of thinking that our sufferings somehow pay for our sins. Suffering perfects our faith, purifying it the way fire removes impurities in gold. Only a faith pruned by trials and purged by difficulty will result in *"praise and glory and honor at the revelation of Jesus Christ"* (1 Peter 1:7).

Peter states that although Christians have not seen Jesus, we *love* Him, *believe* in Him, *rejoice* in Him, and *receive* Him. These four verbs are a beautiful summary of faith; indeed these actions result in *"the salvation of your souls"* (1:9).

The Gospel Message

Verses 3-9 point believers' attention to their future inheritance for encouragement in their present trials. In verses 10-12, however, Peter tells them to look back. *"Concerning this salvation, the prophets ... searched and inquired carefully"* (1:10). Jesus' arrival was not an emergency measure when the human experiment went wrong. Instead, sending His Son was the peak in God's long history of preparation and prophecy extending back to the call of Abraham (Genesis 12:1-3). Even the angels in heaven intensely long to look into the matters surrounding God's good news for humanity.

Personalize this lesson.

✓ Peter was sensitive to his audience's difficult circumstances. He recognized their status as scattered *"exiles of the Dispersion"* (1:1) and acknowledged the struggles they faced, but he encouraged them not to allow their difficulties to rob them of spiritual vitality and inner joy. Instead, he pointed their attention toward the many benefits that were theirs in Christ. Peter saw life's everyday circumstances as insignificant in light of the overwhelming reality of all that God has given to believers. At one time or another, we all need Peter's perspective to deal with life. Ask God to grant you His joy in circumstances that might distract you from the spiritual blessings that are yours in Christ Jesus.

So true, dealing with life is insignificant to the inheritance we are to receive. I have learned that the problems are small compared to the joy, peace, love & hope that we are promised.

When during the day I start going backwards (selfcentered etc. the misery returns.

Starting the day with Jesus & keeping Him by my side all day changes me to loving all that I meet & keeping me stressfree. ♡ Yea Jesus.

Lesson 3

Faithful Children Before a Holy Father
1 Peter 1:13-25

Memorize God's Word: 1 Peter 1:22.

❖ 1 Peter 1:13-25—The Father's Expectations

1. Why do you think verses 13-25 begin with the word *therefore*?

   The old ways & life are gone and the new takes over. Joy not in things but in forever love

2. a. Under the headings below, list the commands and/or expectations Peter gives to God's children. (See also Titus 2:12-14.) God's children are

To Be	To Do
self controlled, say no to worldly passions. To be upright & Godly while we wait	To lead upright & godly lives. until He comes again.

   b. Put the one negative command in your own words.

   Say no to temptation

   c. Which of these commands or expectations offers you the greatest challenge in behaving as a faithful child of God, and why?

   To do, because of my COPD.

❖ 1 Peter 1:13-16—Obedience and Holiness

3. According to 1 Peter 1:14 and Ephesians 2:1-3, what ways of life should be in the past?

    Old ways, doing evil, arrogance greed

4. According to the following verses, what are some advantages of obeying God's Word?

    a. Matthew 7:21 *Go to Heaven*

    b. James 1:25 *God will bless him in everything he does.*

5. a. What one word identifies the *result* of obedience in our lives (1:15-16)?

        Holy

    b. Do you think it is possible to fulfill this command? Why, or why not?

        Yes with prayer and staying away from evil.

    c. In what area of your life do you need to take steps toward greater obedience or holiness?

        I have kept changing, by staying away from evil. Trying to be a good example.

❖ 1 Peter 1:17-21—A Priceless Redemption

6. How does an understanding of God as our *Father* affect the way we live (1:17; Deuteronomy 10:12-13; Ephesians 5:1-2a)?

    To love Him & Worship Him & obey Him Follow Gods example

7. a. *"Ransomed"* (1:18) means to *buy back*. When did God formulate His plan to ransom us?

    When Jesus went to the cross & not with gold or silver. Before the world began

   b. What was the price of that ransom?

    The blood of Jesus

8. What is the result of the ransoming process?

   When we buy back then (it) belongs to us again.

❖ 1 Peter 1:22-25—The Mark of a Christian

9. How are we able to obey the command in these verses to deeply love each other?

   Our souls have been cleansed from selfishness and hatred.

10. From the following verses, why is it important that Christians obey the command to love each other?

    a. John 13:34-35 *It will prove to the world that we are His disciples.*

    b. Colossians 3:12-15 *We are ready to suffer quietly never hold grudges, He forgave us so forgive*

    c. 1 John 3:14-18 *Live without sinning, with others God in our hearts.*

    End Day 4. 20

11. Peter states this command in a deliberate way. What is the difference between *loving* and *loving earnestly from a pure heart*?

    See to it that you really do love each other warmly and with all your hearts. because we have a new life.

12. What do the following verses say about the role of God's Word in the sanctification process?

 a. Psalm 119:9-11 *By reading God's word & following His rules*

 b. John 17:17 *By teaching God's words of Truth*

13. Peter says that people are like withering grass and falling flowers. List as many qualities as you can from verses 22-25 that Peter attributes to God's Word.

love - cleansed - new life - grass burning grown like a flower that droops & fall Good news

14. How has God's Word been a purifying agent in your life? *God's word is truth but it is not just words or a religion it is for the soul and heart loving every one. - Theology -*

15. In what specific way has this week's study caused you to respond to a person or situation differently?

To love those that are not loveable Noise from the young man next door.

Apply what you have learned. Be *"sober-minded… be holy… love one another earnestly from a pure heart"* (1 Peter 1:13, 15, 22). If that standard seems impossible, praise God that He does not expect us to accomplish His commands on our own. His children are engaged in a dynamic relationship with the living, powerful God. Paul's letter to the believers at Philippi reminds us that *"it is God who works in you, both to will and to work for His good pleasure"* (Philippians 2:13). Take time to talk with the Lord daily about what you need from Him in order to live more fully as His obedient child.

& patience - love - joy - peace - hope

Stop worrying about what I have to do, overflow!

Faithful Children Before a Holy Father
1 Peter 1:13-25

Peter points to danger for believers who think they can hold onto their
faith while partially conforming to the surrounding culture. Addressing
the *"exiles of the Dispersion"* (1 Peter 1:1), scattered far from their
homeland, Peter warns these displaced believers against following their
old-life patterns. He reminds them that in matters of faith and conduct
they are responsible to God, for *"He who called you is holy, you also be holy
in all your conduct"* (1:15).

Obedience and Holiness

The word *"therefore"* in verse 13 transitions believers' attention from
their future inheritance promised in Jesus' resurrection (1:3-12) to living
present lives worthy of that promise. Peter's command to *"prepar[e]
your minds for action"* (1:13) points to our attitudes as the root of our
behavior. Our will determines our behavior, and our thinking influences
our wills. Until we *choose* to obey God, our behavior will lack integrity.

Peter tells believers to prepare their minds in two ways. First, believers
should exercise self-control to become submissive to God's will,
becoming *"obedient children"* (1:14). Christians are to transfer their
loyalty from evil desires to obeying a loving Father. The second way
believers prepare their minds for action is by being *"holy"* (1:15). The
word *holy* stems from God's call to Israel to become a pilgrim people,
separated from evil, and joined to the holy God, who wants His children
to reflect His character.

Peter clarifies this idea—of being holy because God is holy—by focusing
on the person of Christ. Peter spoke of believers as *"obedient children"*
(1:14); now he refers to God as a *"Father,"* who *"judges impartially
according to each one's deeds"* (1:17). Genuine faith results in obedient

and fruitful living. Peter's references to God as Father, to being strangers to the world, and to conducting life in fear of God are addressed to believers. Peter is apparently thinking of the judgment of Christians' works. He warns his readers not to assume that their privileged status as God's children gives them freedom to do whatever they desire. Instead, believers are to see themselves as responsible before a holy, loving God— an awesome thought that produces reverent *"fear."* Being in awe of God on our earthly journey is the chief way to *"be holy, because I am holy."* Believers want to be holy because we know that we were not redeemed *"with perishable things … but with the precious blood of Christ"* (1:18-19). Through the sacrifice of Christ's life on the Cross, we were purchased with a redemption that no earthly wealth can buy.

Ransomed means *to buy something back.* Sinners could not accomplish such an act; the payment could be paid only by Someone who had no debt of His own. One of God's prophets described the transaction Jesus made for us: *"He was pierced for our transgressions; He was crushed for our iniquities; upon Him was the chastisement that brought us peace, and with His wounds we are healed"* (Isaiah 53:5). Jesus predicted He would give *"His life as a ransom for many"* (Mark 10:45). He was the totally blameless Passover Lamb (Leviticus 22:19-25). He offered Himself as a sacrifice in obedience to God. In turn, God totally exalts Jesus by raising Him from the dead, *"that at the name of Jesus every knee should bow, in heaven and on earth and under the earth, and every tongue confess that Jesus Christ is Lord, to the glory of God the Father"* (Philippians 2:10-11).

Think about the cost of ransom. Salvation is free to us, but it was paid for by the *"precious blood of Christ"* (1 Peter 1:19). Physically, blood is necessary for life, healing, and restoration. The same is true spiritually: *"Without the shedding of blood there is no forgiveness"* (Hebrews 9:22), and therefore no redemption. Jesus' blood is the price He paid to give us new life. Have you accepted His gift?

A Priceless Redemption

Peter declares that sending the Son to ransom the world was not an afterthought of God or a desperate gamble when all else had failed. Christ was *"foreknown before the foundation of the world,"* but revealed only *"in the last times for the sake of you"* (1:20). Peter reminds his readers that just as the prophets *"were serving not themselves but you"* (1:12) when they prophesied, so God waited until the perfect time to reveal His Son, to raise Him from the dead and to glorify Him *"so [that] your faith and hope are in God"* (1:21).

The Mark of a Christian

The purity of Christians who obey *"the truth"* (1:22) is like the purity of the *"lamb without blemish or defect"* (1:19). This purity leads to *"sincere brotherly love"* (1:22). The New Testament is clear that loving others is the primary characteristic of Christians (1 Corinthians 13), because God *is* love (1 John 4:7-12).

The Enduring Word of God

At the conclusion of this chapter, Peter states, *"You have been born again, not of perishable seed but of imperishable, through the living and abiding word of God"* (1 Peter 1:23). The word translated *"imperishable"* is the same word in Greek that describes the incorruptible inheritance kept in heaven for believers (1:4).

In life's trials, we realize our frailty apart from God. Such troubles can help us see ourselves the way the Bible portrays us—as grass or flowers, weak and vulnerable before the forces of nature. Ironically, seeing our weaknesses helps us appreciate the wonder of the gospel message and God's love for us. God's Word—incorruptible, powerful, transforming, and eternal—comes into our lives and brings a new awareness: Our earthly existence is fleeting, and nothing we can do in our own power will last. But *"the word of the Lord remains forever. And this word is the good news that was preached to you"* (1:25). When the world around us is confusing and uncertain, the Word of God comes to us *"imperishable,"* *"living,"* and *"abiding."* We hear it, receive it by faith, and it produces the certainty of hope (Romans 10:17; 1 Corinthians 15:42-50).

Faith comes from listening to the good news, the good news about Christ.

Personalize this lesson.

☑ Peter considers our status—strangers in the world, God's chosen people, recipients of the new birth and eternal salvation, heirs of God, obedient children, and people redeemed by Christ's precious blood—to be all the motivation Christians need to live obedient, holy, and distinctive lives. Circumstances easily paralyze us, but we must learn to think, choose, and respond in godly ways. Christianity means relationship—a personal relationship with the living, unconditionally loving God, and deep, loving relationships with people.

Does your faith impact every dimension of your life—your personality, relationships, values, priorities, work, leisure, family life, and ability to cope with whatever circumstances God ordains and permits in your life? Allow His Word to accomplish His intended purpose: *"My word that goes out from My mouth … shall not return to Me empty, but it shall accomplish that which I purpose, and shall succeed in the thing for which I sent it"* (Isaiah 55:11).

Send out His word & it always produces fruit.

A hunger for God's word

Living Stones in God's Temple
1 Peter 2:1-10

Memorize God's Word: 1 Peter 2:9.

❖ 1 Peter 2:1-3—Conditions Hindering Spiritual Growth

1. *excuses*
   worry

   a. Peter specifies five sins that endanger spiritual health and growth, personally and corporately. List and define each sin, and tell how it affects us and our relationships with others, especially in the church.

Sin	Definition	Effects
1) Dishonesty Hatred			Malice
2) Jealousy			deceit
3) Deception			hypocracy
4) Envy			envy
5) Fraud			slander

   arrogance
   b. If you detect any of these sins in your heart, list several *practical ways* you can deal with them.

   _____

   _____

   _____

❖ 1 Peter 2:1-3—Conditions Stimulating Spiritual Growth

2. What specific characteristic of a newborn baby does Peter encourage God's children to imitate?

   Cry for salvation as a baby cries for milk

3. What does God intend to happen as a result of a believer seeking spiritual food?

   Fullness of salvation.

4. Share a personal example of how a "taste of the Lord's goodness" motivated you toward greater spiritual growth.

   Betty Sue & Robin Hunter coming to the house & showing film on our wall - Northside = Parabino

❖ 1 Peter 2:4-8—The Church: Built on the Cornerstone

5. What can you discover from the context of this passage regarding the identity and nature of the *"living Stone"* (2:4; see also Acts 4:8-12)?

   Jesus is the basis of the church, the people are the rest of it. (Jesus is the capstone, people the rest)

6. How does Jesus' parable in Luke 20:9-19 add to your understanding of the living Stone?

   The church is Jesus & the people.

7. a. Why do people stumble over and reject Christ? (See also Romans 9:30-33; 1 Corinthians 1:18-25.)

   Because they follow the law not faith

"I have put a rock in the path of the Jews."

b. Are the reasons people stumble any different today than in Peter's time? Explain.

No they still believe that just being good is the way. Believing in Jesus is the way!

c. Can anyone be neutral about Jesus Christ? Why, or why not? Give Scripture to support your answer.

1 Cor. 19 God says, I will destroy all human plans of salvation no matter how wise they seem to be, & ignore the best ideas of men, even the most brilliant of them." God's wisdom

❖ 1 Peter 2:4-10—The Church: Living Stones and Holy Priests

8. How does a person become a *"living stone"*?

As we come to Him we become, living stones we are the church.

9. What does the metaphor of *"living stones … being built up as a spiritual house"* imply about each *"living stone"* (2:5; see also 1 Corinthians 3:16-17; 6:19-20)?

We together are the house of God & the Spirit lives with us. We are the stones

10. What does Ephesians 2:19-22 tell us about the *"spiritual house"* into which believers are being built?

We are now members of God's own family, His household, not strangers

11. Although Jesus Christ made the ultimate and final sacrifice for sin, God accepts spiritual sacrifices from His children. Choose two of the following references to explain what sacrifices please Him in individual believers' lives and in the church as the *"holy priesthood"* (2:5).

a. Psalm 51:16-17 *A broken Spirit, remorse & penitence/A right attitude*

b. Romans 12:1-2 *The renewing of the mind & total commitment to God*

c. Ephesians 5:1-2 *A self giving life in Christ God is love.*

d. Hebrews 13:15-16 *Continually offer to God a sacrifice of praise.*

❖ 1 Peter 2:9-10—The Church: The People of God

12. What do Exodus 19:5-6 and Deuteronomy 7:6 add to Peter's declaration in verse 9 that believers *"are a chosen race, a royal priesthood, a holy nation, a people for His own possession"*?

God has chosen us. He loves us unconditionally. He chooses us not because of our merit.

13. Considering the circumstances (1:6-7), what do you think Peter is trying to accomplish in writing to these people?

testing them, these are hard times for them. learn they are more precious than gold.

14. If you are trying to fulfill God's call in your life, share what you have experienced as a result.

I am learning to love everyone. I am a priest to forgive & forget. To serve others

---

Apply what you have learned. Is your church an instrument for God's purposes in your community? Are you doing your part as one of His living stones? Pray for the body of Christ—locally and globally—to be and to do all that God intended.

Living Stones in God's Temple
1 Peter 2:1-10

In chapter 1, Peter set before believers the *"living hope"* (1:3) of their inheritance in Christ and challenged them to behavior that is worthy of such an inheritance. In 2:1-10, he describes the nature of the church in which believers participate as *"living stones"* (2:5).

Spiritual Growth

If Christians are to progress in our faith, we must cultivate conditions that make growth possible. One condition is a clean break with anything contrary to God's will. We are to be done with everything that is harmful to our faith. Peter lists five attitudes that poison faith: *"all malice and all deceit and hypocrisy and envy and all slander"* (2:1). These five sins undermine and destroy Christian fellowship. Each of these sins needs to be uprooted.

Peter's readers were evidently recent converts, for he refers to them as *"newborn infants"* (2:2), a common expression in Judaism for Gentile converts. A newborn has an instinctive desire for its mother's milk, and newborns in faith just as surely *"long for the pure spiritual milk."* Spiritual milk refers to God's Word. An eager desire for God's Word is as vital to growing in faith as hunger for milk is to the physical growth of a baby. We may think spiritual maturity can happen quickly, but the fact is that the Holy Spirit is in the process of forming and transforming us. Life is a journey to Christ-likeness.

Building the Church

A dominant theme of 1 Peter is that believers are to conform to Jesus' image. Peter now presents the idea in architectural imagery; Christ is the living cornerstone of the temple. Christians are the living building blocks. As *"living stones"* (2:5), believers must be cut and polished. Even

Christ is a *"living"* stone in this respect, for He, too, *"learned obedience through what He suffered. And being made perfect, He became the source of eternal salvation to all who obey Him"* (Hebrews 5:8-9).

Think about the ways in which God *"cuts and polishes"* His people. Perhaps this concept was in Peter's mind when he wrote that *"you have been grieved by various trials, so that the tested genuineness of your faith—more precious than gold that perishes though it is tested by fire—may be found to result in praise and glory and honor at the revelation of Jesus Christ"* (1:6-7). God allows nothing in your life to go to waste. As you face trials, does it help to know God is using them to make you more like Jesus?

In verse 4, Peter directs attention to Jesus, the chief cornerstone of the church (Ephesians 2:20). Ironically, the stone God designed to determine the dimensions of the house was *"rejected by men."* Nevertheless, it is *"chosen"* by and *"precious"* to God and the perfect example for each brick in the *"spiritual house."*

The imagery in verses 5 and following is corporate, not individual, which means that we can become what God wills us to be only if we are with other believers. The church is the living community of faith where we hear the word of salvation, receive our call, discover our gifts, grow in faith, and—when necessary—receive correction and discipline.

A house is built of many bricks, not one. God's Word calls Christians to fellowship as *"living stones,"* with Christ and with one another. *"Living stones"* symbolize the spiritual nature of the church. The temple in Jerusalem was constructed of stone and masonry, but the living stones of the church are a *"spiritual house."* Priests in Israel had to be descendants of Aaron from the tribe of Levi, but all the stones of the church are part of a *"holy priesthood"* (2:9). The old covenant sacrifices included killing unblemished animals, but our offerings are *"spiritual sacrifices"* (2:5).

Christ: A Blessing or an Offense

The New Testament reveals that there is no neutral zone with respect to Jesus Christ (Matthew 12:30). The apostle Paul told the Corinthians that the gospel is either the power of God to those who believe it or foolishness to those who do not; it is never a matter of indifference (1 Corinthians 1:18). Peter's letter includes Old Testament quotations to make the same point. All three quotations in 1 Peter 2:9 use the *"rejected stone"* theme. To those who believe, Christ's worth is inestimable. Some believers today worry about how their Christianity will affect their social or professional status. Nevertheless, the meaning of verse 7 reinforces the preceding quotation: No one who trusts in Christ will be put to shame.

Not everyone believes, of course. If we will not accept God's Word as a light to our path (Psalm 119:105), then we find that such rejection becomes a stumbling block. Is it God's will that some disbelieve and stumble? The conclusion of 1 Peter 2:8 might suggest so: *"They stumble because they disobey the word, as they were destined to do."* However, a careful reading reveals that God does not cause people to stumble, but that stumbling is the inevitable result of disbelief. God does not predestine the disobedience, but He does predestine the penalty for it.

The People of God

God chose us; our lives are a priestly sacrifice; and we are a people belonging to God in the most intimate way. Wonderful as all this is, it is a prelude to our proclaiming *"Him who called you out of darkness into His marvelous light"* (2:9). The important thing is not who we are, but making known who God is and what He has done. The gospel is that good news!

Verse 10 concludes the discussion about the community of faith: *"Now you are God's people; once you had not received mercy, but now you have received mercy."* This echoes the Old Testament prophet Hosea. Moved by love and mercy, he reclaimed his faithless wife as an illustration of God's reclamation of Israel. Peter applies the words to the church, made up of Jews and Gentiles.

Personalize this lesson.

☑ As living stones in God's temple, we were not meant to inhabit God's house; we *are* God's house. Or, perhaps it might be more appropriate to refer to it as *God's mobile home*, for it is not confined to one place. As each of us—as living stones—go about our daily business, we carry with us the Chief Cornerstone. If you have trusted Christ, then you are a living stone, wherever you are. Have you thought about ways in which you can better reflect the Chief Cornerstone as you go about your daily business?

Stay with Him & be like Him. Love, Peace
Hope, Joy. We are not perfect. We
still suffer & grow. Deeper & deeper
Faith. Continue to grow those
building blocks.

The Testimony of the Servant Life
1 Peter 2:11-25

Memorize God's Word: 1 Peter 2:21.

❖ 1 Peter 2:11-12—A Life of Abstinence

1. a. State the two exhortations—one negative, one positive—
        Peter uses to begin this section.

        *Stay away from evil pleasures. They
        fight against our souls*

    b. How does his reminder of their status (1:1; 2:11) relate to
        those commands? (See also John 17:14-19.)

        *Johns prayer is not that they stay away
        but that you protect us from the evil
        one.*

2. From Romans 13:12-14 and Galatians 5:16-26, expand Peter's
    meaning in verse 11.

    a. What are some specific examples of the *"passions of the flesh"*
        from which Christians are to abstain?

        *Wild parties, getting drunk, or adultery
        lust, fighting or jealousy. (Put on
        the armor of God.*

    b. What are the consequences of *"gratify[ing] the desires of the
        flesh"*?

        *They will not inherit the kingdom
        of God.*

c. What commands or suggestions does Peter give for how to
"abstain from the passions of the flesh"?

Stay away from the evil pleasures

❖ 1 Peter 2:11-12—A Life of Godliness

3. a. What does verse 12 reveal about the surroundings of Peter's
audience?

They are unsaved

b. How does he suggest they respond to these circumstances?
Why?

*Suspicious of you & talking against
us. They will praise God for our good works.*

4. According to Philippians 2:14-16 and Titus 2:7-8, what are
some of the characteristics of those who "keep [their] conduct ...
honorable" and the resulting effects on others?

*lead clean innocent lives as children
shine like a beacon of lives.*

5. Have you asked God to help you live in such a way that the
unbelievers who observe your life glorify God? If you have not
done so, will you do so now?

*We are to live pure lives to exemplify
God.*

❖ 1 Peter 2:13-17—A Life of Submission

6. *Submit* means *to yield in surrender, compliance, or obedience.* In
what aspects of your life do you find submission difficult?

Family

7. From Peter's perspective, as well as Paul's exhortations
    (Romans 13:1-7; Titus 3:1-2), how does God expect Christians
    to treat their governing leaders? Why?

    To obey our governing leaders & officers.
    Because God has chosen them.

8. a. How would you explain Peter's word of caution in 1 Peter 2:16?

    We are free from the law but not free
    to do wrong

    b. How do verses 16-17 teach us balance between becoming a
        "doormat" and rebelling against authority?

    Show respect for everyone. Love Christians
    everywhere. Fear God & honor the Government.

❖ 1 Peter 2:18-21—A Life of Servanthood

9. Summarize principles of servanthood from these instructions to
    1st-century slaves:

    a. 1 Peter 2:18-21 *respect to your masters*
        patient

    b. Ephesians 6:5-8 *Obey your masters & give*
        them your very best. Work w/ gladness
        as though working for Jesus all the time.

10. Do the same principles apply to Christians in 21st-century? Why,
    or why not?

    Yes, when working for Jesus, it
    is a joy

❖ 1 Peter 2:21-25—Living in His Steps

11. To what are Christians *called*?

    To suffer

12. a. As Peter recalls Jesus' circumstances and His responses (see also Isaiah 53), what does he imply about what Christians of his day are facing?

The same as Jesus faced.

b. How does Christ's suffering relate to a Christian's submission in a trying situation?

We must always call on Him for help.

c. What are the eternal effects of Christ's sufferings?

He is the one to carry the load.

13. a. Instead of retaliating, what does Jesus *choose* to do (2:23)?

He left His case in the hands of God.

b. How could adopting a similar response affect your attitude toward your suffering?

We just ask Him to take it & He does.

Apply what you have learned. Note Paul's challenge in Philippians 2:5-11: *"Have this mind among yourselves, which is yours in Christ Jesus."* What attitudes do you need to change to be more like Christ? Confess anything in your life you would be ashamed for God to see (1 John 1:9) and turn from it. Knowing that walking *"in His steps"* will lead to submission, perhaps even suffering, are you willing to follow Jesus regardless of the route? Never hesitate to ask for His help.

The Testimony of the Servant Life
1 Peter 2:11-25

More than any other circumstance or situation, unjust suffering gives believers the opportunity to imitate the example of Christ, who suffered for us.

Ambassadors to Foreign Lands

In 2:11 Peter addresses his readers as *"beloved,"* embraced by God and bound to Him and one another by His unconditional love. Peter also calls us *"sojourners and exiles,"* because we have not reached our final destination. As such, we share a harmony with the Lord and one another that we do not share with our worldly environment. Ambassadors cannot afford to let their host country's attractions distract them from serving their government; neither can Christians allow fleshly, sinful desires to jeopardize their souls. *"Abstain from the passions of the flesh,"* writes Peter, *"which wage war against your soul."* In the original language, the verb tense of the word abstain indicates continued abstaining; we ought to keep on abstaining.

By standing strong against such desires, we demonstrate the kind of conduct that disarms the pagan world's opposition. Peter does not say *if* they accuse you of wrongdoing. Opposition *will* come. The most virtuous life is no insurance against accusations. Jesus Himself was the object of spite, malice, and undeserved martyrdom. Yet the power of a good life can transform maligning God's people into glorifying God *"on the day of visitation"* (2:12). That day may refer to the final judgment or the Second Coming of Christ, but it may also mean the day on which nonbelievers are converted to faith, at which time they will *"glorify God."*

Submission to Authorities

Peter asserts that submission to human authorities is an ethical good. Both Peter and Paul believe God ordains human governments. More importantly, they agree on the divinely ordained purpose of governments, which is *"to punish those who do evil and to praise those who do good"* (2:14; Romans 13:3-4). Government does not possess absolute sovereignty (which inevitably results in tyranny), but governments have the responsibility, as do their citizens, to do what is right. The two apostles agree that Christian citizens should not give their service to government out of obligation, but as free people.

Totalitarianism holds that the purpose of subjects is to serve the state; if subjects are of no service, they can be discarded as so much obsolete equipment. Christianity says all people have value, whether they are useful to the state or not, because God creates people in His image. God's Word teaches that the purpose of human life is to glorify God. Christians know that God alone is Lord. Once that fact is established, our relationship to other authorities is clarified. God puts political leaders in office, and they are worthy of our respect and honor, but not of our ultimate allegiance and worship.

Think about your attitude toward your country's leaders. God's Word suggests a positive way to relate to those in authority: *"I urge that supplications, prayers, intercessions, and thanksgivings be made for all people, for kings and all who are in high positions"* (1 Timothy 2:1-2). Why? So *"that we may lead a peaceful and quiet life, godly and dignified in every way."*

"Honor everyone. Love the brotherhood. Fear God. Honor the emperor" (1 Peter 2:17). Peter does not offer a theology of government so much as practical advice about Christian citizenship. The primary result of obeying the authorities is that *"by doing good you should put to silence the ignorance of foolish people"* (2:15). Peter is concerned that believers' behaviors bring neither the gospel nor themselves into disrepute. Christians are free, but we must not use our freedom as a pretext or *"cover-up for evil"* (2:16). As God's gift, freedom is rightly employed when people are servants of God, not slaves to their *"passions of the flesh"* (2:11).

The Suffering Servant

Submission to political authorities is not the only form of submission Peter expects of believers. In verse 18, he uses the same verb (*hypotassein*, meaning *to submit or to be subject to*) to refer to servants and masters. In the ancient world, large numbers of people lived in varying degrees of servitude, and slaves began to make up a considerable proportion of the church. Spiritual guidance for them was important to the early church.

Not only are slaves to submit to their masters, they are to do so regardless of the master's character. Inevitably, slaves suffer injustice. The idea of respectfully submitting to an unjust master irritates our sense of justice. However, in choosing to submit respectfully because God has instructed them to do so, slaves are following Christ's example, and God will bless them: *"For this is a gracious thing, when, mindful of God, one endures sorrows while suffering unjustly"* (2:19).

Suffering gives believers a visible means of demonstrating faith, love, and loyalty to Christ. Beyond that, in some unexplained way, suffering confirms God's existence and the certainty of His concern and thus results in inner peace and conviction. Peter develops this theme through the rest of the chapter by applying several images of the Suffering Servant from Isaiah 53 to the model and example of Jesus Christ. In Greek, each of Peter's statements in verses 22-24 begins with a pronoun referring to Christ.

Peter intends the references from Isaiah 53 to apply also to his readers. The references to verbal abuse in this letter— *"When He was reviled, He did not revile in return; when He suffered, He did not threaten"* (2:23; see also 2:12, 15; 3:9, 16; 4:4, 14)—reveal that Christians were abused and harassed in Peter's day. The reference to Jesus' implicit trust in God (He *"continued entrusting Himself to Him who judges justly"* [2:23]) is likely an exhortation to Peter's readers not to lose faith in the midst of prolonged injustice. His words were timely then, and they are timely today.

Finally, Peter concludes in verse 25 with the certain hope and antidote for every problem. Although his readers are like errant sheep (Isaiah 53:6), in Jesus we find the *"Shepherd and Overseer"* of our souls.

Personalize this lesson.

☑ Peter emphasized the believer's responsibility to live a life of integrity and obedience before the Lord, regardless of the reactions of others and the resulting circumstances. In what current circumstances do you need to trust God to be the Shepherd of your soul? Will you be like the supreme Suffering Servant who *"continued entrusting Himself to Him who judges justly"* (1 Peter 2:23)?

Today as I read & study the Bible. I have found the truth. Over the many years I have lived I have listened to good people say & talk about our Lord. There have been so many contradictions that I learned the Bible had, has the only truth. In many cases the world tells us one thing & the Bible another. Our young people are so vulnerable, I know I've been there. Please Lord keep me from judging, self-centered, arrogant. Learn to love thy neighbor as thyself.
Bless Washington D.C. & New York city.
Please stop them from killing babies.

Jesus Christ: From Servant to Sovereign
1 Peter 3

Memorize God's Word: 1 Peter 3:15.

❖ 1 Peter 3:1-7—Godly Wives

1. To what does the word *likewise* (3:1) refer?

   The wives quiet behaviors, can be used by God

2. In Peter's day wives were subject to their husbands' authority in the same manner as that of a household servant. What aspects of the principles Peter teaches might be thought progressive in that day?

   Husband & wives are partners.

3. From the passage, what qualities does God value in a woman?

   Godly lives. Quiet spirit—

4. Do you think this passage overlooks or justifies men oppressing, exploiting, or abusing women? Why, or why not?

   Women are doing what God tells us to do, we will be blessed, as partners no one gets this blessing

❖ 1 Peter 3:1-7—Marital Harmony

5. In a marriage between a believer and an unbeliever, how is a Christian wife supposed to respond to her unbelieving husband?

The same, quiet, loving then actions will speak louder than words

6. Have you witnessed the effectiveness of these principles, either personally or in the experience of a friend or relative? Please share.

Betty Sue & Robin Hunter, Examples of working together & for others

7. Peter gives instruction to husbands who want to be sensitive and obedient to God's design for marriage. (See also Ephesians 5:21-33.)

   a. How should a godly husband treat his wife?

   Love her as part of himself. Love her as Christ loved the church

   b. What spiritual impact do his attitudes and behavior have?

   Have a gentle & quiet spirit. Be beautiful inside your hearts.

❖ 1 Peter 3:8-12—Relational Harmony

8. a. Peter's instructions are relevant to Christians today. List the phrases that describe what a Christian should be and do to maintain harmony in relationships.

   We are to be like one big happy family loving one another with tender hearts & humble minds.

   b. According to Peter, what are the benefits of living this way?

   God will bless us.

9. How are we to respond to evil and insults (3:9; see also Luke 6:27-31)?

   Turn away from evil & do good. Don't repay evil for evil.

10. How are we to respond to deceitful conversation (3:10; see also Ephesians 4:29; James 3:9-12)?

    Keep control of the tongue.

11. What do the following verses say about developing the virtue of pursuing goodness, peace, and righteousness?

    a. 3:11-12 *Turn away from evil & do good. Try to live in peace & do good.*

    b. Philippians 4:8-9 *Fix your thoughts on what is true good & right.*

❖ 1 Peter 3:13-17—The Fellowship of Suffering

start 8/31/16

12. a. What advice does Peter give to Christians who encounter suffering in spite of their commitment to a godly lifestyle?

    We are to be envied. Trust self to God, do what is right

    b. What additional encouragement do Jesus' words give us in the Beatitudes (Matthew 5:1-12)? *Blessed are the peacemakers because they are the children of God*

    Humble, kind & merciful, pure hearts

13. How does Peter say we can be effective in sharing and defending our faith?

    Quietly trust yourself to Christ. Then do it in a quiet & respectful way.

They were beaten by the council [handwritten note in margin]

14. How do the following passages confirm Peter's conviction that suffering for righteousness' sake is good?

a. Acts 5:41 _God counted them worthy to suffer dishonor in His name._

b. Romans 8:18, 35-39 _What we suffer for now is nothing to the glory we will receive later._

❖ 1 Peter 3:15-22—The Lordship of Christ

15. How can setting apart Christ as Lord in your heart (3:15) affect your Christian lifestyle? Give an example from your own life.

If Gods love shows thru, His love will silence others.

16. How does the picture of Christ in this passage give you hope for specific sufferings or difficulties in your life?

It is not about me, trust in Him, He has suffered for me

Apply what you have learned. How do you respond to injustice? Often our human reaction to unfair treatment is "Why me?" or "I don't deserve this." Instead of reacting that way, why not ask God to help you face unjust and difficult circumstances from the perspective of the hope that is within you because you have set apart Christ as Lord in your heart? You know He will not let this pain be wasted. Ask Him how He wants you to respond and what He wants you to learn from the experience.

Jesus Christ: From Servant to Sovereign
1 Peter 3

The discussion of wives and husbands in 3:1-7 completes the section on servanthood that began in 2:11. The middle part of the chapter picks up the refrain of suffering for the sake of doing good, first introduced in chapter 2. Then the chapter concludes with a powerful testimony to Christ's sovereignty.

Advice to Wives and Husbands

In addressing wives and husbands, Peter now applies the principle he gave in 2:18 regarding slaves submitting to masters. Peter addresses wives and slaves similarly because a wife who became a Christian in the ancient world faced a situation similar to a slave who became a Christian. Women were subject to their husbands' authority. If a husband became a Christian, he brought his wife (and family) into the church as a matter of course. However, a wife who became a Christian had no authority over her husband. If he remained a pagan, her faith could jeopardize the marriage.

Many a believing wife probably thought, as did many believing slaves, that conversion marked the end of submission to a non-believing husband or master. Peter's advice follows the thought he began in 2:12—if anything can cause a change of heart within pagans in authority, it is the godly conduct of those in subordinate roles. Let unbelievers simply *"see your respectful and pure conduct"* (3:2). Unbelieving husbands who *"do not obey the word … may be won without a word by the conduct of their wives"* (3:1).

The statement to *"be subject to your own husbands"* (3:1) is significant. Peter directed his rule on submission specifically to wives and their own husbands. This verse does not justify men oppressing or exploiting women, or specifically, husbands exploiting wives—a point Peter will make again in verse 7.

Peter's reference to hair, jewelry, and clothing is intended to teach that true beauty must be cultivated inwardly. The ultimate adornment in God's eyes is *"the imperishable beauty of a gentle and quiet spirit"* (3:4). The beauty of an inner spirit is unfading and eternal, and in God's eyes it is more valuable than the most priceless jewels and perfume.

Offensive though it may be to some people, the Bible praises Sarah for obeying her husband. The story of Sarah's submission to Abraham when they were in Egypt (Genesis 12:10-20) has sometimes been wrongly used to insist that women submit even when they are asked to do things that are illegal, immoral, or dangerous for them or their children. <u>Obeying and pleasing God always takes precedence over obeying and pleasing men.</u>

To balance the perspective on Christian marriage, the apostle turns his attention to husbands, assuming a partnership between husband and wife in Christian marriage. Christian husbands are to be considerate, a word in Greek that excludes all violence and abuse. Believing wives are *"heirs with you of the grace of life"* (3:7), and therefore destined by God for the same inheritance as believing husbands.

The Fellowship of Suffering

The theme of harmony within a marriage proceeds naturally to the wider theme of harmony within the church, which Scripture views as an extended family. The rule in verse 9 of refusing to respond to evil with evil is an echo of the example of Jesus and His teaching: *"Love your enemies, do good to those who hate you, bless those who curse you"* (Luke 6:27-28). Peter says, *"To this you were called, that you may obtain a blessing"* (3:9). The Christian life is a combination of suffering and blessing, cross and crown.

If we do the things 1 Peter 3:8-9 tells us to do, the blessing we inherit (verse 9) will keep our tongues from evil, help us to turn from evil and do good, and move us to pursue peace. Modern culture may confuse and reverse the two, but good and evil are exclusive opposites. Good must always be pursued—not only when it is convenient. Thus, be *"zealous for what is good"* (3:13).

The Christian's first witness to the unbelieving world is that of good conduct. Although verbal witness is secondary, Peter instructs, *"Always [be] prepared to make a defense to anyone who asks you for a reason for the hope that is in you"* (3:15). Believers are to be ready to speak on behalf of the faith. The answer must not attack or coerce, but be made with *"gentleness and respect"* and with a *"good conscience"* (3:16). The malicious slander of unbelievers should be without grounds, so that those who seek to discredit Christians will have reason to feel shame.

Think about the implication of 1 Peter 3:15. In spite of any circumstances, believers are to demonstrate an unquenchable hope that motivates others to ask about that hope. If someone were to ask you about Jesus, how well *"prepared"* are you to share the gospel as *"a reason for the hope that is in you"*?

Christ, Lord of Heaven and Earth

Peter gives a summary of the person and work of Christ, who is not simply an example of righteousness, but the means of it: *"Christ also suffered once for sins, the righteous for the unrighteous, that He might bring us to God"* (3:18). On the Cross, Jesus took the sins of the world on Himself and granted His righteousness to those who accept God's gift.

Biblical scholars provide various interpretations of the strange passage about Jesus' preaching to *"the spirits in prison, because they formerly did not obey"* (3:19-20). Surely Peter did not intend to confuse our thinking, but to strengthen our faith and to help us understand that Jesus is Lord of the entire cosmos.

Peter's words about water in verses 20-21 include two figures of speech. The water of the Flood in Noah's time speaks of judgment; the water of Christian baptism symbolizes Christ's death, burial, and resurrection. Participation in baptism identifies us with Christ in all that He has done for us. Baptism is our pledge to keep a *"good conscience"* (3:21). Such a commitment is reasonable because Christ, who died for us, is now seated in the place of divine authority—*"with angels, authorities, and powers having been subjected to Him"* (3:22).

Personalize this lesson.

☑ Jesus Christ, the Suffering Servant, is the supreme example of a righteous response to insults, pain, and evil as He *"continued entrusting Himself to Him who judges justly"* (2:23). Likewise, God calls all who are His children to place ourselves—in the midst of our circumstances—in the secure hands of a loving and powerful heavenly Father. When we truly do that, we realize, as the apostle Paul did, that our *"light momentary affliction is preparing for us an eternal weight of glory beyond all comparison"* (2 Corinthians 4:17), and that eternal perspective can comfort us in any trial, whether it is brought by people or by circumstances.

Good Managers of God's Bounty
1 Peter 4:1-11

Memorize God's Word: 1 Peter 4:8.

❖ 1 Peter 4:1-11—The Mark of a Disciple

1. What questions come to mind when you hear of Christians suffering for their faith?

    Family can hurt the most.
    Old age alone

2. From John 15:16-21, why should Christians expect persecution?

    Because we believe in the Father

3. Compare the way pagans live (4:3) with the way Christians are supposed to live (4:7-10).

Pagans	Christians
Life running after evil desires.	*anxious to do the will of God.*

❖ 1 Peter 4:1-2—Identification With Christ

4. Why should we have the same attitude as Christ?

    He who has suffered in his body is done with sin

5. According to the following verses, what results should suffering
    produce in our lives?

    a. Romans 5:1-5 *perseverance, peace with God*
        character, hope

    b. James 1:2-4 *perseverance must complete*
        its work so that we may be mature

    c. 1 Peter 1:6-7 *We must suffer to refine*
        our faith.

6. How do believers make it obvious they have *ceased from sin*?
    Arm ourselves with the same attitude
    as Christ

7. All people die. What is unique about Christ's death? (See Peter's
    references to Christ's death in chapters 1-3 and other Scriptures.)
    Christ chose to die for us to believe.

(margin handwritten notes:) *Father decided* *Jesus suffered* *Holy Spirit moved it along* *in faith*

❖ 1 Peter 4:1-6—Choosing to Live God's Way

8. a. Like Peter, Paul described the "before and after" of a life-
        changing encounter with God. Using 1 Peter 4:1-6 and
        Ephesians 2:1-10, compare the following:

The lifestyle and state of a person without God	The lifestyle and state of a person committed to God
wild parties, sin, idols	*Helping others*

    b. God's role in the life of:

A Believer	An Unbeliever
God is rich in mercy	

sex, sin, lust, getting drunk, wild parties, drinking bouts, worship of idols

9. What do you think motivates non-Christians to pressure those around them to approve of and participate in an ungodly lifestyle?

   feel good, wanting to be their friend,

10. What do the following verses say about every person's accountability before God?

   a. Jeremiah 17:10 *The Lord searches all hearts & deepest motives so He can give to each his right rewards. How he's lived.*

   b. Romans 2:1-12 *We are all sinners & must learn to change all ways that are evil.*

   c. 1 Corinthians 3:10-15 *The foundation is Jesus Christ. & how we have built on Him.*

   d. 2 Corinthians 5:10 *We will all stand before Jesus our lives laid bare. thoughts??*

11. Do you find the thought that you are accountable to God frightening or encouraging? Why?

   Both - frightening because I may have missed them & encouraging because I have changed.

❖ 1 Peter 4:7-11—Anticipating the End of All Things

12. a. Peter is convinced that *"the end of all things is at hand"* (4:7). What specific instructions does he give to believers?

   Be earnest thoughtful men of prayer

   b. Which of these instructions particularly challenges you? Why?

   My calling - Hospitality - I'm having a hard time doing anything. But am trying

   Larry's surgery

❖ 1 Peter 4:7-11—Gifted to Serve

13. What can you learn about the source and purpose of spiritual gifts from the following verses?

    a.   1 Peter 4:7-11 *God has given us special gifts be sure to use them to help each other.*

    b.   Ephesians 4:7-16 *Because of what Christ has done we have become gifts to God. We are to praise God & give glory to Him.*

14. Considering the circumstances of Peter's audience, why do you think he writes about spiritual gifts?

_____

_____

15. In 1 Peter 4:11, Peter mentions speaking and serving gifts. *Speaking* gifts probably include teaching, exhortation, and prophecy; *serving gifts* probably include helps, encouragement, mercy, giving, etc. Why are these two areas important to the emotional and spiritual health of the church body in any age?

_____

_____

16. In verse 8, do you think Peter is encouraging Christians to "sweep sin under the rug"? (See also Proverbs 10:12.)

_____

_____

Apply what you have learned. More than 2,000 years have passed since Peter wrote his letter to prepare and equip believers for suffering, knowing that *"the end of all things is near"* (1 Peter 4:7). Ask God to empower His people to live *"in order that in everything God may be glorified through Jesus Christ. To Him belong glory and dominion forever and ever. Amen"* (4:11). What will you ask Him specifically to do for you so He can receive glory?

Good Managers of God's Bounty
1 Peter 4:1-11

Believing that a commitment to Christ can be blended with worldly values is <u>dangerous</u>. Peter urges believers to recognize the truth: Life in Christ is new and different; we are now trustees of God's grace.

The Difference Faith Makes

"Since therefore Christ suffered in the flesh," Peter writes, *"arm yourselves with the same way of thinking"* (1 Peter 4:1). Christian faith begins in the historical fact that around AD 30 Jesus suffered and died at the hands of His own people and the ruling Romans in the land of Israel. That fact alone is not extraordinary; all people die. Jesus' death has significance when we interpret it according to God's purpose. <u>God the Son died as a sin offering for the world.</u> His crucifixion is a personally applicable, saving event we receive by faith alone. Suffering is the inevitable consequence of the sins of the world, which God dealt with in Christ in order to redeem His creation.

Taken alone, the remainder of verse 1—*"for whoever has suffered in the flesh has ceased from sin"*—appears to suggest that our sufferings are capable of atoning for our sins. Scripture offers no support for this conclusion. The phrase rightly refers to believers whose suffering draws them closer to God and helps change their evil human desires. <u>Human suffering cannot atone for our sins; Christ's payment for sin is sufficient.</u>

God's will stands in contrast to worldliness, to *"doing what the Gentiles want to do"* (4:3). Pleasures such as *"sensuality, passions, drunkenness, orgies, drinking parties, and lawless idolatry"* may seem enticing, but such behavior is a *"flood of debauchery"* (4:4), a cesspool of evil. Peter's readers—having been pulled from the swamp of immorality—are likely being viciously attacked by their former associates. The new believers pay a big price for their changed behavior.

God's will is eternal; *"human passions"* are temporary and destined for God's judgment. Unbelievers may be surprised at Christian self-control and may even ridicule it, but they should recognize that they, too, *"will give account to Him who is ready to judge the living and the dead"* (4:5). Knowing that God holds us accountable in the future, Christians follow His will in the present. Doing so, we begin to see more and more similarity between what we are now and what we will someday become: *"We know that when He appears we shall be like Him, because we shall see Him as He is"* (1 John 3:2).

Different interpretations of 1 Peter 4:6 are possible, but one seems most plausible. *"For this is why"* does not look back to verse 5 and the judgment of living and dead unbelievers. It looks forward, in verse 6, to the word *"that."* Deceased believers had an opportunity to hear and believe the gospel while they were still living. Therefore, although people might have judged them and even taken their bodily lives, God's judgment will determine the final destiny of unbelievers (4:5) and believers (4:6).

Servants and Stewards of God's Grace

In saying that *"the end of all things is at hand"* (4:7), Peter has at least three aspects of salvation in mind, through which God will ultimately subject all things to Himself. First, Christ's resurrection overcame death. Second, the establishment of Christ's rule has begun in His exaltation and enthronement (3:22). Third, all hostile powers have not yet been fully subjected, but await the final appearance of the Chief Shepherd (5:4). Christians live in confidence of Christ's final victory over evil, even before that victory is fully carried out.

The latter half of 1 Peter 4:8 has been interpreted in various ways. Some take the statement that *"love covers a multitude of sins"* to mean that love does not find fault with others but prays for those who sin. The Greek word Peter uses twice is *agape*, God's kind of love. God's love alone, demonstrated in the sacrificial death of His Son (1 John 3:16), atones for sin. But Christians are called to imitate His love (1 Corinthians 13). Our best attempts are only dim images of Jesus' unconditional love, but our mission is to try to reflect the gracious way God always deals with us.

Think about love as a believer's most important calling—*"above all,"* writes Peter (4:8). Jesus commanded His followers to love one another; love is how people know we are His followers (John 13:34-35). Love for one another is proof that we love and obey God, for *"he who does not love his brother whom he has seen cannot love God whom he has not seen"* (1 John 4:20).

When Peter urges Christians, *"Show hospitality to one another without grumbling"* (1 Peter 4:9), he means it as a concrete expression of love. Hospitality was a particularly important gift during the 1st century, when there were no hotels and the few inns were costly, dirty, and even dangerous. The writer of the letter to the Hebrews instructed, *"Do not neglect to show hospitality to strangers, for thereby some have entertained angels unawares"* (13:2). Paul also urged believers in Rome and those who served with Timothy to use their gift of hospitality for the benefit of the church at large.

Peter concludes with what has been his leading thought, to *"serve one another, as good stewards of God's varied grace"* (1 Peter 4:10). Christians are equipped for service with a spiritual gift at the moment they accept Christ. The important thing is not the gift but its purpose, and that is to serve. Serving is not simply something Christians ought to do; it is something we must do as stewards or trustees of God's grace.

Good stewards consciously affirm God's way as our own way and make God's life our own life. God's language becomes our language; all our service is service to God. The purpose of our speech is to glorify God, and the source of our service is the strength and power of God. *"Whatever you do, in word or deed, do everything in the name of the Lord Jesus, giving thanks to God the Father through Him"* (Colossians 3:17).

Personalize this lesson.

☑ What should God's people be doing as we await the Lord's return? *"Be self-controlled and sober-minded for the sake of your prayers … keep loving one another earnestly…. Show hospitality to one another … serve one another"* (1 Peter 4:7-10). Many secular psychologists, as well as Christians, teach that one of the best antidotes for depression (which often accompanies trials) is to serve others, as Peter advised. If you are struggling through difficult trials, will you ask God to lead you into a ministry of service to others?

The Fires of Adversity
1 Peter 4:12-19

❖ **1 Peter 4:12-19—Suffering and Faith**

1. How do you think most people view suffering and hardship?

   _____

   _____

2. Which of Peter's words or phrases remind you of specific times of suffering, testing, or trials in your life?

   _____

   _____

3. What divine resources has God made available to you and what can He accomplish in your life when you go through testing?

   _____

   _____

❖ **Surprised and Tested by Suffering**

4. In 1 Peter 4:12, Peter refers to the *"fiery trial"* his readers are suffering. From the passage's context, what is he referring to?

   _____

   _____

5. According to Peter, how should we *not* react to suffering?

   _____

   _____

6. What do you learn about testing from the following verses?

   a. Malachi 3:1-4 _____

   _____

   b. 1 Peter 1:7_____

   _____

7. How have you seen God refining your faith or the faith of someone close to you through trials?

   _____

   _____

   _____

   _____

8. What judgment might Peter be predicting (4:17; see also 1 Corinthians 3:10-15)?

   _____

   _____

   _____

9. a. What is the purpose of the judgment of believers referred to in Matthew 16:27 and 2 Corinthians 5:10?

   _____

   _____

   b. Should believers be worried about this event (1 John 4:16-18)? Why, or why not?

   _____

   _____

10. What are the desired results and potential rewards of this judgment? (See also 1 Corinthians 9:25; 2 Timothy 4:8.)

    _____

    _____

    _____

❖ Rejoicing in Suffering

11. Why are Christians to exhibit joy in times of suffering? (See also Philippians 3:7-11; James 1:2-4.)

_____

_____

_____

_____

12. What important distinction does Peter make about suffering (1 Peter 4:14-16; see also 2:19-23)?

_____

_____

_____

13. From Acts 5:27-42, what specific ways has Peter personally experienced the principles he teaches:

    a. participation in the sufferings of Christ (4:13)?

    _____

    _____

    b. praise to God in the midst of suffering (4:13, 16)?

    _____

    _____

    c. practical provision and protection from God (4:19)?

    _____

    _____

14. How do Peter's concluding instructions in verse 19 both comfort and challenge suffering Christians?

_____

_____

_____

_____

Apply what you have learned. Recall a personal experience of physical, emotional, or relational suffering. Given your present understanding of God's perspective and purpose for suffering, identify the positive effects of that experience. Take time to thank God for His purpose, protection, and provision in all aspects of your life, and commit your future to your faithful Creator. He loves you deeply.

The Fires of Adversity
1 Peter 4:12-19

Peter declared earlier that believers should rejoice in their new birth, in their great inheritance, and in God's shielding power *"though ... you have been grieved by various trials"* (1:6). He now repeats and completes that theme, which has been developed throughout the epistle: *"But rejoice insofar as you share Christ's sufferings"* (4:13). Peter reveals that suffering plays an essential role in the life of faith and is not simply the result of unbelievers' malice. It is a necessary process to which God subjects the church and believers in order to temper and refine their faith. The test or examination is already underway, for *"judgment ... begin[s] at the household of God"* (4:17).

Rejoicing in Hardship

"Do not be surprised at the fiery trial when it comes upon you to test you.... But rejoice" (4:12-13). The word for *fiery* means *a testing of metals by fire* (Proverbs 27:21). Just as in the physical world fire refines metal, in the spiritual world trials refine faith. Trials reveal whether our hearts are sincere and upright before God, or hardened and resistant. Peter insists that Christians should not be surprised by fiery trials. His Gentile readers (see 4:3) may have been in particular need of this reminder because, unlike their Jewish-Christian counterparts, they had been part of their culture's status quo and were unaccustomed to opposition.

A major test of true faith in Christ is choosing to rejoice in suffering, according to Peter; he says we *"share Christ's sufferings"* (4:13). As in Philippians 3:10, Paul's exhortation here to *"participate"* means more than simply enduring or holding out. Amazingly, the fellowship of the sufferings of Christ is not intended to produce a grim countenance, but joy and rejoicing, for believers will *"rejoice when [Christ's] glory is revealed."*

First Peter 4:13 again reminds us that true faith presents a challenge as well as a promise. This humanly impossible challenge is to be willing to suffer with Christ and to rejoice in doing so. We understandably do not want to suffer, and we struggle to find the joy in suffering that Peter speaks of. However, our faith the promise that suffering on Christ's behalf brings the deepest possible fellowship with Him makes this joy possible.

Peter's readers were subjected to insults and abuse *"for of the name of Christ"* (4:14), and were regarded as atheists and enemies of the state for failing to worship the imperial gods, including the emperor. Nevertheless, Peter encourages them to turn to the comfort and strength of Holy Spirit. With the words, *"the Spirit of glory and of God rests upon you,"* Peter reminds the struggling believers that the very Spirit who equipped and sustained Jesus for ministry indwells their hearts as well, empowering them as they face these hardships.

Peter reminds his readers that it is not a blessing to suffer for criminal activity. The only suffering Peter upholds as good and *"gracious ... in the sight of God"* is to *"do good and suffer for it"* (2:20). Peter urges believers not to feel shame if we suffer because of our faith in Christ; instead, we should offer up praise to God that we are called Christians and made the target of such persecution.

Until this point, Peter has addressed the suffering his readers have undergone as a result of antagonism from non-Christians. In verse 17, however, he mentions another reason: *"It is time for judgment to begin at the household of God."* This idea was not novel to Peter. The prophets had unexpectedly spoken of God's judgment beginning not with the pagan nations, but in Israel's temple sanctuary (Jeremiah 25:29; Ezekiel 9:6). *"Who can endure the day of His coming?"* Malachi asked. *"Who can stand when He appears? For He is like a refiner's fire ... [He] will draw near to you for judgment"* (Malachi 3:2-5).

It probably shocked Peter's readers, who were already victims of persecution, to hear that God's judgment would fall on them before it fell on their antagonists. However, they needed to understand that God holds His own people accountable and expects them to maintain a higher standard of righteousness than their surrounding culture. The Lord who founded and sustains the church is the same Lord who judges His own to cleanse, strengthen, and perfect them.

Think about Peter's warning if you hear someone preach an easy Christianity, proclaiming that health and wealth are the signs of God's blessing. Jesus stunned His disciples by stating that faith does not bring an exemption from pain, but a cross to bear (Mark 8:34). God remains present in the trials of daily life as well as in our victories. Our response to adversity reveals whether we walk the easy way or take up our cross and continue on the road that Christ traveled before us, allowing God to use our problems and our pain to transform us into His image.

If judgment begins with the household of faith, *"What will be the outcome for those who do not obey the gospel of God?"* (4:17). When Peter rephrases Proverbs 11:31, asking *"if the righteous is scarcely saved,"* he does not mean believers stand a slim chance of salvation. Rather, if it takes a tough practice to get his *good* players in shape, what will the coach have to do with the bad ones to get them in a condition to be useful in the game of life?

Whatever our circumstances, believers *"entrust their souls to a faithful Creator while doing good"* (4:19). Distress should not cause believers to doubt God and His goodness. Peter's consideration of trials and hardships falls between two great assurances, one at the beginning (1:6) of the epistle and one at the end (5:10), that God in His providence sets limits to human suffering. First Peter 4:19 is, moreover, the only instance in the New Testament where God is called *"Creator"* (in Greek). As Creator, God knows the purpose for which He has made all things, and how to restore them when they have gone awry. We can trust Him to work in and through our suffering, knowing that He is faithful to His promises.

Personalize this lesson.

☑ As God's children, we are called to commit ourselves to our *"faithful Creator and continue to do good"* (1 Peter 4:19). The greatest testimony of faith is to trust God in the midst of despair, to fight the good fight when the battle seems lost, to keep doing good when evil seems to triumph. The principles regarding suffering in Peter's teachings are reminiscent of David's words in Psalm 37:3-9. As a reminder and an encouragement, read these verses and insert your name before each imperative (trust, do, dwell, enjoy, delight, commit, etc.).

Advice to Christian Leaders
1 Peter 5

Memorize God's Word: 1 Peter 5:6-7.

❖ 1 Peter 5:1-4—Shepherding God's Flock

1. What credentials does Peter claim as he addresses church *"elders"* (leaders)?

   _____

   _____

2. a. From this passage, list some "nots" and "buts" of leadership.

"not ..."	"but ..."
(1)	
(2)	
(3)	

   b. As you view yourself in light of these verses, do these principles of servant-leadership challenge or affirm your serving and/or leading style? Please explain.

   _____

   _____

   _____

   _____

3. Peter calls Jesus the Chief Shepherd (5:4). Read Jesus' description of Himself in John 10:1-18. Make a descriptive list of the roles and responsibilities of shepherds and sheep.

Shepherd	Sheep

4. Read Acts 20:25-35. Why was mature and healthy leadership such a critical issue to Paul and Peter as they ministered to the early church?

_____

_____

5. Read Luke 9:28-36. What does Peter know concerning the *"glory"* about which he writes (1 Peter 5:1, 4)?

_____

_____

6. What does it mean to you that you are *"a partaker in the glory that is going to be revealed"* (5:1; see also Philippians 3:20-21; Colossians 3:1-4)?

_____

_____

_____

❖ 1 Peter 5:5-7—Humbling Ourselves

7. a. What significance do you find in Peter's directive to young men?

_____

_____

   b.   What command does Peter address here to all believers regardless of office or age?

    _____

    _____

8.   How is humility important as a character trait of God's children? (See also Proverbs 11:2; 16:18; and Philippians 2:5-8.)

    _____

    _____

9.   Anxiety often results from our inability or unwillingness to humbly trust God. How do the following verses speak to you about this lack of trust?

   a.   Psalm 37:3-11 _____

    _____

    _____

   b.   Proverbs 3:5-6_____

    _____

    _____

   c.   Philippians 4:4-7 _____

    _____

    _____

❖ 1 Peter 5:8-9—Facing Spiritual Warfare

10. a.   What do Peter's words here suggest to you about Satan's nature and tactics? (See also Genesis 3:1-5; Matthew 4:1-11.)

    _____

    _____

    _____

   b.   How does Peter suggest we combat our enemy, Satan?

    _____

    _____

11. In Ephesians 6:10-18 we read of resources available as believers face spiritual warfare. What phrases communicate the attitudes and actions with which we are to resist Satan?

_____

_____

12. How does knowing that your brothers and sisters throughout the world are undergoing the same kind of sufferings encourage you to stand firm in your faith?

_____

_____

13. What conclusion can you draw from verses 8-9 concerning the source and nature of the sufferings about which Peter wrote in his letter?

_____

_____

❖ 1 Peter 5:10-14; 2 Corinthians 4:16-18—Concluding the Letter

14. Using Peter's benediction (5:10-11) and 2 Corinthians 4:16-18, how would you summarize God's view, purposes, and role in human suffering?

_____

_____

_____

Apply what you have learned. Reread 1 Peter 1:3-7; 2:19-24; 3:14-18; 4:12-19; and 5:10-11. If someone asked you to explain the biblical, Christian view of suffering, what would you say?

Advice to Christian Leaders
1 Peter 5

Shepherding God's Flock

Peter's main purpose in writing his first epistle has been to encourage Christians who are suffering, but he also offers a concluding word to church leaders. Using shepherding imagery, he exhorts elders to tend God's flock in the manner of the *"Chief Shepherd,"* Jesus Christ. Peter makes only two claims for himself (5:1), both designed to connect with his readers. He appeals to the elders on the basis of shared experience, as *"a fellow elder."* To those undergoing hardships, he speaks as *"a witness of the sufferings of Christ."* Peter does not call their attention to his own sufferings, which might serve to build him up, but to Christ's sufferings. Finally, he shares the same hope of *"the glory that is going to be revealed"*—what he saw foreshadowed in Jesus' transfiguration (Mark 9:2-7) and resurrection.

Following Peter's denial of Jesus (John 18:15-27), the risen Lord visited him beside the Sea of Galilee and, instead of rebuking him, commissioned him to shepherd His flock (John 21:15-17). Shepherding was an apt metaphor for church leadership. Shepherding does not justify control and domination, for the flock is *"the flock of God"* (5:2), not the shepherd's. In discipline and in doctrine, the shepherd must lead, not drive; protect, not seclude; inspire, not manipulate; and feed, not exploit.

In 1 Peter 5:2, Peter speaks of *"exercising oversight."* Pastoral duties are described in three sets of opposites: *"not under compulsion, but willingly"*; *"not for shameful gain, but eagerly"*; *"not domineering over those in your charge, but being examples to the flock"* (5:2-3). God's character provides our model for Christian leadership. God freely bestows His presence and good gifts; He desires responses made freely out of love for Him.

Professed Christians coercing others in God's name is a particularly grating incongruity.

The gospel does not end with the present; it points our perspective to the future, *"when the Chief Shepherd appears"* (5:4). The image of God as Israel's Shepherd extends back to the nation's early days (Psalm 23:1; Isaiah 40:11). Here it is used of the Arch Shepherd, who is *above* elders as the archetype of church leadership and *before* them as their goal and reward in glory. Shepherds belong to the Chief Shepherd; they are accountable to Him for fulfilling their duties; and they look to Him for their final hope, *"the unfading crown of glory"* (5:4).

Think about the spiritual leaders in your life. What would happen if you began to pray faithfully for them, using 1 Peter 5:1-5 as a foundation for your prayers? Perhaps God has called *you* to a leadership role. Do you lead with the servant-heart described by Peter? What an impact the Chief Shepherd's flock would have in our world if the shepherds and the sheep lived in mutual service and humility.

Humbling Ourselves

At the end of this part of his letter, Peter tells all Christians to *"clothe yourselves, all of you, with humility toward one another"* (5:5). The word for *humility* (*tapeinos*) in verses 5-6 means not simply to humble oneself, but also to accept being humiliated as a result of following Christ's way. God rewards those who admit their poverty and need of Him. Christians must consciously remember that God's *"power is made perfect in weakness"* (2 Corinthians 12:9). We experience His power as we acknowledge our weakness.

Facing Spiritual Warfare

Knowing God cares should not lull believers into complacency. We must *"be sober-minded; be watchful,"* because *"the devil prowls around like a roaring lion, seeking someone to devour"* (5:8). The metaphor of the devil prowling around like a roaring lion reminds us that our adversary is a spiritual opponent. A lion on the loose is an effective word picture of evil's destructive power. Just as a lion's roar frightens its prey, Satan "roars" to intimidate believers into accepting his lies. Rather than cowering in terror of Satan, we must *"fear [God] who can destroy both soul and body in hell"* (Matthew 10:28).

Peter exhorts Christians to resist this enemy, *"firm in your faith"* (5:9). Christians are called to watch out for the devil and to resist him; God will do the rest. As believers, we are never alone in our struggles. God is with us, and so are others: *"The same kinds of suffering are being experienced by your brotherhood throughout the world."*

Concluding the Letter

This thought about the prevalence of Christian suffering leads Peter to conclude with a benediction in verses 10-11. Note the four terms at the end of verse 10. They are all cast in the future tense, testifying to the absolute surety of God's benevolence. The first term, to *"restore"* to wholeness, is the Greek word that means *to set aright* (e.g., a broken bone), or *to mend* (a torn net). The second phrase, *"strengthen,"* (from which steroids is derived), means *to strengthen* or *to set firmly* (as in concrete). The third, *"confirm,"* means *to make strong*. The fourth, *"establish,"* means *to lay a foundation, to set girders deep to support a superstructure*. God's grace and calling to glory operate through suffering. Suffering infused by grace strengthens us, making us *more* than we were, fit partners for God in glory (2 Corinthians 4:16-18).

"She who is at Babylon" (5:13) is a puzzling reference. Many Jews (and surely some Christians) were still living in Babylon at the time of this epistle, and it is not impossible that this reference is to Mesopotamian Babylon. More likely, the reference is to Rome, which by the late 1st century was symbolized as Babylon because of its oppressive policies toward Christians.

"Mark, my son" (5:13) does not mean a biological son, but a son in faith, perhaps even brought to faith by Peter. The Mark to whom Peter refers is likely the author of the Gospel of Mark, the John Mark of Acts 13:13, and Paul's one-time companion.

Peter's first letter speaks at length of trial, persecution, and suffering. Nevertheless, the closing word is *"Peace to all of you who are in Christ"* (5:14). Not human struggle, not even the struggle of faith, but Christ's presence and peace is the final word of this epistle.

Personalize this lesson.

☑ The Greek word Peter used that is translated *"restore"* in 1 Peter 5:10 is the same Greek word (*katartizo*) that Paul used in Ephesians 4 when he wrote of equipping the saints: *"And He gave the apostles, the prophets, the evangelists, the shepherds and teachers, to* **equip** *the saints for the work of ministry, for building up the body of Christ"* (Ephesians 4:11-12). In order to be *equipped* to build up the body of Christ, we need to be *restored*. Restored from what? From the doubts stirred up by our *"adversary, the devil,* [who] *prowls around like a roaring lion"* (1 Peter 5:8). And that restoration from doubt is exactly what Peter says God will do: *"And after you have suffered a little while, the God of all grace, who has called you to his eternal glory in Christ, will Himself restore, confirm, strengthen, and establish you."* Have trials buffeted you and stirred up doubts about your faith? If so, embrace the truth that the God of all grace will restore and establish you; and when He does, you will be better prepared to help in equipping other saints *"for the work of ministry."*

The Human Response to God's Initiative
2 Peter 1

Memorize God's Word: 2 Peter 1:3.

❖ 2 Peter 1:1-21—Our God's Powerful Initiative

1. a. How do grace and peace come into our lives?

   _____

   _____

   b. How does this motivate you?

   _____

   _____

2. What phrase identifies the means by which we can experience all we need for life and godliness? (See also Jeremiah 9:23-24.)

   _____

   _____

3. Recalling the admonition in 1 Peter 1:14-16, what do verses 3-4 reveal about the *possibility* of living a godly life?

   _____

   _____

❖ 2 Peter 1:1-9—The Believer's Faithful Response

4. a. From verses 1-4, in what ways has God taken the initiative in His children's lives?

   _____

   _____

b. What phrase communicates the desired *intensity* of our response to His initiative?

_____

_____

5. a. List the things we are to add to our faith, making brief comments about the importance of each or about your understanding of each.

Add to your faith	Importance or understanding
1.	
2.	
3.	
4.	
5.	
6.	
7.	

b. Verses 5-7 show that developing the virtues that produce a fruitful Christian life is a process. Explain the significance of the order in which Peter lists them.

_____

_____

_____

❖ 2 Peter 1:5-11—Living Out the Faith

6. What insights does Romans 8:28-30 provide into God's ultimate purpose(s) in calling us to growth and maturity in our faith?

_____

_____

_____

7. What are the causes and results of spiritual immaturity?

_____

_____

8. What assurances are ours as we commit ourselves to spiritual growth and maturity?

_____

_____

9. Explain the relationship between true knowledge of Christ and a godly lifestyle. (See also Matthew 7:15-23; Colossians 1:9-12.)

_____

_____

❖ 2 Peter 1:12-21—Established in the Truth

10. What is Peter's purpose in writing this letter?

_____

11. Why is timing so critical for him?

_____

_____

12. What do these verses reveal about Peter's attitude toward life and death?

_____

_____

13. a. What specific aspects of Christ's glory were revealed at the Transfiguration (see Matthew 17:1-8 and 2 Peter 1:16-18.)?

_____

_____

b. Despite the fact that the manifestations of the Transfiguration are mainly visual, what most impacts Peter?

_____

_____

c. What apparently prompts Peter's reference to this event?

_____

_____

❖ 2 Peter 1:16-21—The Witness of the Word

14. a. What word picture does Peter use to encourage us to *"pay attention"* to God's Word?

_____

_____

   b. What does this image suggest regarding the practical value of the Word in our lives?

_____

_____

15. What is particularly significant to our understanding of Scripture? (See also John 14:25-26.)

_____

_____

16. What do you learn about the work of the Word as revealed in Hebrews 4:12-13?

_____

_____

 Apply what you have learned. Do you believe God has given *you* everything *you* need to live the Christian life? If you were to draw more fully on His power, what changes would you desire to see in your faith as well as your lifestyle? Talk to God about this with an expectant heart.

The Human Response to God's Initiative
2 Peter 1

Peter's first letter encouraged churches in Asia Minor that were suffering under persecution. His second letter, on the other hand, focuses on false teachers and their attempts to discredit Christian faith because of the delay in Christ's return.

Authorship and Salutation

Second Peter bears the name of *"Simon Peter"* (1:1) as author, states that it was written by an eyewitness of the Transfiguration of Jesus, and even alludes to the author's upcoming death.

Peter identifies his audience simply as those who *"obtained a faith of equal standing."* This letter begins with Peter's humility (*"Simon Peter, a servant"*) and with the idea that believers deserve equal honor with the apostle himself. Equality is based on the fact that faith is *"obtained"* as a gift of grace, not earned or inherited through privilege. The result is an undeserved *"righteousness"* that comes from God.

A Faithful Response to God's Call

The letter begins on a majestic note: *"His divine power has granted to us all things that pertain to life and godliness"* (1:3). That is an absolute claim. The godliness, obedient conduct, and holiness that Peter calls for are grounded in this power. God would not command such things unless they were in line with His will and made possible by His divine power. We can trust God to provide us with the divine power to become holy, as called for in 1 Peter 1:16: *"Be holy, because I am holy."*

Think about the statement "but I'm only human." Because God *"has given us everything we need for life and godliness,"* we have no excuse for blaming our frail humanity when we fail to live a life that pleases Him. We may be disobedient, but we are not powerless. He offers this power for our daily lives. Praise God!

Second Peter 1:3-4 tell us that God *"called us to His own glory and excellence,"* and progress in such goodness is made possible by *"His precious and very great promises."* God intends His call and promises to restore humanity to creation's original standards, enabling believers to *"become partakers of the divine nature."* But this restoration is not automatic. We must respond to God's love in Christ if we want to escape *"from the corruption that is in the world because of sinful desire."*

According to verse 5, faith is a gift; however, it is a gift that must be nurtured and cared for. Peter lists the supply line of faith in a chain of qualities (verses 5-7): *"virtue ... knowledge ... self-control ... stead-fastness ... godliness ... brotherly affection ... love."* The list begins with *"virtue."* Virtue precedes knowledge, implying that character is a prerequisite to learning. Self-control and perseverance are necessary to godliness, which in turn paves the way for brotherly kindness and love. According to 1 Corinthians 13, love is the supreme virtue, but there is no shortcut to attaining it. Christian maturity is a step-by-step process, not an instant attainment.

We are saved by faith, but we remain *"ineffective or unfruitful"* (1:8) unless we cultivate behavior that corresponds to faith. In chapter 3, Peter speaks of knowledge that is necessary to correct error and falsehood. But knowledge is barren and sterile without goodness, self-control, godliness, and love. A Christian who does not realize that the purpose of knowledge is to produce virtue and be used for good *"is so nearsighted that he is blind, having forgotten that he was cleansed from his former sins"* (1:9). When virtue and knowledge join faith, two things happen: *"Your calling and election are* "confirm[ed],*" and "there will be richly provided for you an entrance into the eternal kingdom of our Lord and Savior Jesus Christ"* (1:10-11).

The Witness of the Spoken and Written Word

Progress in faith depends on a support system. Effective preaching and teaching enable us to hear, understand, and receive the Good News. But Peter attests in verses 12-15 that faith is strengthened through reminders, admonitions, and encouragement. Our human hearts are slow to understand and quick to forget. The Christian life consists not simply in knowing the truth, but in being *"established in the truth that you have"* (1:12).

The phrase *"I know that the putting off of my body will be soon"* (1:14) refers perhaps to Peter's awareness that he would die a martyr's death. The transmission of the gospel into the lives of others ensures that our ministry will outlive our brief earthly existence, for *"after my departure you may be able at any time to recall these things"* (1:15).

The gospel consists not of *"cleverly devised myths"* but a testimony of *"eyewitnesses of His* [Christ's] *majesty"* (1:16). Christianity is not a myth, nor even primarily an ethical code. It is the account of a historical occurrence where God, working through His Son, made it possible for the world to be reconciled to Himself. It is eyewitness accounts, which later became incorporated into written accounts, so that when the eyewitnesses died, their witness endured.

Peter elaborates on Christ's *"majesty"* in 1:17-18 by reference to the Transfiguration (Matthew 17:1-5). He doesn't testify to what he saw but rather to what he heard: *"We ourselves heard this very voice borne from heaven, for we were with Him on the holy mountain."*

Second Peter 1:19 reaches back to God's word to Moses and the prophets, its fulfillment in Jesus Christ, and its passage through the apostolic witness, both spoken and written. This prophetic word is both the foundation and confirmation of faith. It is *"a lamp shining in a dark place, until the day dawns and the morning star rises in your hearts."* When Christ returns for the final judgment, we shall know by sight what we now know only by faith.

Chapter 1 closes by considering that *"lamp,"* which is identified as *"Scripture"* (1:20), as something originating with God. *"First of all, ... no prophecy was ever produced by the will of man, but men spoke from God as they were carried along by the Holy Spirit"* (1:20-21).

Personalize this lesson.

✓ Peter begins this letter of caution regarding false teachers and heretical teachings by reminding his readers of the truth in which they are *"established"* (1:12). The believer who is unconditionally committed to a growing faith and godly living is much less susceptible to false teachers and their teachings than the Christian who is indifferent or lukewarm to the claim of God on his life. How, specifically, are you building on the sure foundation of God's Word? Remember that Peter wrote that *"you will do well to pay attention"* (1:19).

Lesson 11

False Teachers
2 Peter 2

❖ **2 Peter 1:20–2:9—A Stern Warning**

1. *Summarize* in one or two sentences the warning contained in this passage.

    _____

    _____

    _____

    _____

2. On what historical facts does Peter base his exhortation to the 1st-century believers?

    _____

    _____

3. The Old Testament contains numerous references to false prophets and false shepherds. From the following passages, identify the issues significant to God as He spoke through His prophet Jeremiah.

    a. Jeremiah 6:13-15 _____

    _____

    _____

    b. Jeremiah 14:14-16_____

    _____

    _____

❖ 2 Peter 2:1-9—Be Alert to Dangers

4. List ways in which false teachers are dangerous.

_____

_____

_____

_____

5. What point is Peter making by using Old Testament examples (1:4-9)?

_____

_____

6. Read Psalm 92.

    a. What is the basis for the blessing of which the psalmist sings?

_____

_____

    b. What is the basis for the judgment?

_____

_____

    c. What principles do Psalm 92 and 2 Peter 2:4-10 teach?

_____

_____

_____

7. a. Using a dictionary, define *heresy* (2:1).

_____

_____

    b. What heretical teaching was particularly damaging to the Christians Peter addresses?

_____

_____

8. What is your response to 2 Peter 2:9?

_____

_____

❖ 2 Peter 2:10-22; Jude 1-25—Characteristics of False Teachers

9. Record your observations of characteristics of false teachers, using these categories.

Personalities and Lifestyles	Doctrines and Beliefs	Ministry Styles and Tactics

10. a. What appeal might teachers with these characteristics have for Christians today?

_____

_____

    b. In what ways are the messages of false teachers invalidated by their spiritual condition (2:19-22) and their eternal destiny (2:1, 9, 17)?

_____

_____

❖ Characteristics of Godly Teachers and Leaders

NOTE: The following Scriptures were chosen from among many because of their direct reference to teachers.

11. What characteristics should be evident in the lives and ministries of godly teachers?

    a. 2 Corinthians 4:1-2, 5 _____

_____

_____

   b. 2 Corinthians 6:3-7 _____

_____

_____

   c. 1 Thessalonians 2:3-12 _____

_____

_____

❖ Our Response to False Teachers

12. If you were ever influenced by false teaching, please share about it. Identify the characteristics of the teacher, content of the teaching, its appeal to you, and how you dealt with it.

_____

_____

13. Read 2 Timothy 2:22-26; 4:1-5. What directions does Paul give Timothy about the proper response to false teachers and false teachings?

Positive	Negative

Apply what you have learned. What steps can you take to know better how to discern truth and error in spiritual teaching? Think of those who teach you. Will you commit yourself to pray for the teachers and leaders in your life, that their public ministry and personal lifestyle would be characterized by integrity and purity? They need your prayers.

False Teachers
2 Peter 2

This second chapter of 2 Peter, like Jude's letter, is a carefully thought-out, strongly expressed condemnation of false teachers. These two New Testament authors agree on the danger of false teaching and the judgment against those who perpetrate it. This subtle, but fatal, deception is a distortion of divine revelation and spiritual truth.

Rescue of the Just From the Company of the Wicked

In this letter, Peter speaks several times of a proper knowledge of the gospel as the standard by which false teachers are condemned. From Israel's earliest days *"false prophets also arose among the people"* (2:1). It should come as no surprise that false teachers arose within the church. Peter accuses them of *"denying the Master who bought them."* These leaders smuggle in *"destructive heresies"* and set them up alongside truth.

Any church can become complacent about wrong doctrine, supposing that what Christians believe is less important than how they feel and act. This is a mistaken judgment because *"many will follow their sensuality, and because of them the way of truth will be blasphemed"* (2:2).

What will become of those who twist the truth and lure believers into tragic choices and circumstances? Second Peter 2:4-10 gives examples of God's judgment. The list begins not with men, but with angels who seduced earthly maidens (Genesis 6:1-4). The context refers to angelic adversaries and corrupted spiritual forces. God's judgment against spiritual rebellion is decisive and unsparing: the sinning angels are sent to hell and confined to *"gloomy darkness,"* farthest removed from the light of God's presence.

God *"did not spare the ancient world … when He brought a flood upon the world of the ungodly"* (2:5). However, even in His judgment,

God demonstrates grace by saving the family of Noah, a *"herald of righteousness."* Throughout Scripture, God tempers His judgment with grace. This principle was also illustrated by the fact that when God turned *"the cities of Sodom and Gomorrah to ashes He condemned them to extinction"* (2:6). Yet from among the inhabitants of these wicked cities, God saved Abraham's nephew, Lot, a *"righteous man"* (2:8). The Old Testament depicts Lot as one who collaborated in his generation's depravity (Genesis 19). However, although he did not openly condemn that depravity, he was evidently not content with it. He was *"greatly distressed by the sensual conduct of the wicked"* (2:8). Whatever the degree of Lot's righteousness, God had mercy on him, because *"the Lord knows how to rescue the godly from trials"* (2:9).

Think about God's proactive support of His children. *"The eyes of the LORD run to and fro throughout the whole earth, to give strong support to those whose heart is blameless toward Him"* (2 Chronicles 16:9). Picture God intentionally looking for those who are committed to godliness so that He can fully strengthen and support them. Will you choose to make that commitment, knowing He will strengthen and support you as well?

God holds *"those who indulge in the lust of defiling passion and despise authority"* (2 Peter 2:10) accountable at the Day of Judgment. *Authority* could be translated *lordship*, referring to those who disdain God's sovereignty. Peter implies that those who reject God's grace will not escape His judgment.

The Guilt of Unrighteousness

Peter describes the false teachers as *"bold and willful"* and *"not tremble[ing] as they blaspheme the glorious ones, whereas angels, though greater in might and power, do not pronounce a blasphemous judgment against them before the Lord"* (2:10-11). Jude 8-10 clarifies the meaning of this verse; Michael contests with the devil over Moses' body and has more respect for the devil than the false teachers have for God and His angels. *"Pleasures"* and *"revel"* (2 Peter 2:13) indicate lack of discipline. The Greek word used here for *"pleasures"* carries the sense of *deceptive pleasures* as opposed to *God-ordained pleasures.* They are *"blots and blemishes,"* precisely the opposite of the *spotless* and *blemish-free* character of Christians approved in 2 Peter 3:14. *"They have eyes full of adultery"* and they *"entice unsteady souls"* (2:14).

Orthodoxy follows a *"right way"* (2:15), but heresy follows an easy, impulsive way. Peter cites *"Balaam, the son of Beor"* (see Numbers 22) as an example of this error. Enticed by dishonest gain, Balaam was willing to curse the living God. So, too, are false teachers willing to teach their scandalous doctrines for financial gain. Balaam *"was rebuked for his own transgression; [by] a speechless donkey"* (2 Peter 2:16). Even beasts are of better use to God than are false teachers! As *"waterless springs and mists driven by a storm"* (2:17), false teachers quench no thirst and produce no harvest. Nothing could be worse than pastors who entice new converts, *"barely escaping from those who live in error"* (2:18). Yet that is exactly what false teachers do.

Every impostor since the serpent's sly discussion with Eve (Genesis 3) has promised freedom: an appeal to man's desire to assert himself over God. The false teachers *"promise them freedom, but they themselves are slaves of corruption. For whatever overcomes a person, to that he is enslaved"* (2 Peter 2:19). Sin seizes control of those who indulge their baser nature. Had the false teachers once been true believers who then fell away from God, or had they once appeared to be believers—people who knew *about* the Lord though they never actually *knew* Him? The text doesn't say they are actually Christians, so they appear to be false teachers who only know *about* the truth. They have managed temporarily to correct their pagan lifestyle, but now revert to their true nature. They have forsaken their knowledge of *"our Lord and Savior Jesus Christ"* and *"are again entangled in [the corruption of the world]"* (2:20). God prefers the genuine doubt of the honest unbeliever to the pretense of a hypocrite who professes Christianity in name only (Revelation 3:15-16). For those who pretend, *"it would have been better for them never to have known the way of righteousness than after knowing it to turn back from the holy commandment,"* says verse 21. Those who forsake the faith reveal that they hope to build their house quickly on sand rather than on the true bedrock.

Personalize this lesson.

✓ Chapter 2 paints a grim picture of false teachers and their ultimate fate, and it concludes with two repulsive proverbs in verse 22. In what areas of your life could you incorporate a more active search for truth and ground your theology more solidly in Scripture? Believers possess the calm assurance of our position and power in Christ, knowing that His Word provides the standard against which to measure other teachings. Though it may be frightening, particularly when we stand alone, we must *"always* [be] *prepared to make a defense to anyone who asks … for a reason for the hope that is in you; yet do it with gentleness and respect"* (1 Peter 3:15).

The Promise of the Lord's Return
2 Peter 3

Memorize God's Word: 2 Peter 3:11-12a.

❖ **2 Peter 3 (focusing on verses 1-2)—Reasons for Writing**

1. a. What reasons does Peter give for writing this letter?

    _____

    _____

    _____

    b. What definition and value does Philippians 4:8-9 give to the first of Peter's reasons?

    _____

    _____

2. Given the threat of false teachings, why are his stated reasons for writing so important?

    _____

    _____

    _____

3. What do Ephesians 2:19-20 and 2 Timothy 2:19 add to your understanding of the benefit of knowing and doing right?

    _____

    _____

    _____

❖ 2 Peter 3:3-7—The Challenge of the Last Days

4. How does 2 Peter describe the scoffers and their message? (See also Jude 18-19.)

_____

_____

5. To what does Peter attribute their error?

_____

_____

6. As you read the following descriptions of *"the day of judgment and destruction"* (2 Peter 3:7), contrast the characteristics and destiny of:

	Ungodly Scoffers	Righteous Believers
a. Romans 2:5-11		
b. 2 Thessalonians 1:5-11		
c. Revelation 21:5-8		

❖ 2 Peter 3:3-15a—The Promise of the Day of the Lord

7. How does God's view of time differ from ours? (See also Psalm 39:4-6; 90:4-6.)

_____

_____

8. How should God's perspective on time affect the believers' attitudes regarding the issues raised by scoffers? (See also Hebrews 10:35-39; James 5:7-9.)

_____

_____

9. How does 2 Peter 3:10 say the *"day of the Lord"* will come?

    _____

    _____

10. Record additional insight about the significance of that
    description of the Day of the Lord using:

    a. Acts 1:6-8 _____

        _____

    b. 1 Thessalonians 5:1-6_____

        _____

11. According to this passage in 2 Peter, what is the destiny of the
    world as we know it?

    _____

    _____

12. a. What question should the reality of these future events
        prompt in our minds?

        _____

        _____

    b. What answers does 2 Peter 3 give us?

        _____

        _____

13. What is the object of the believer's anticipation? (See
    Revelation 21:1-5.)

    _____

    _____

❖ 2 Peter 3:14-18—Living in Readiness

14. Peter lists three actions believers can take to maintain a state of
    spiritual readiness. Record each and give an example of *how* a
    Christian might accomplish each on an ongoing basis.

    a. Verse 14_____

b.   Verse 17 _____

c.   Verse 18 _____

15. a.   What specific problem does Peter address in verse 16?

_____

_____

b.   What are the potential consequences of misusing Scripture?

_____

_____

❖ 2 Timothy 3:1-17—Living in Victory

16. What principles of spiritual growth and maturity do you find in these verses?

_____

_____

17. Reread 2 Timothy 3:16-17 and think back over your study of 1 and 2 Peter.

a.   Note at least one thing it *taught* you.

_____

_____

b.   How did the study give *"training in righteousness"* or equip you for living in your world?

_____

_____

 Apply what you have learned. If Jesus Christ returned today, would He find you being *"diligent to be found by Him without spot or blemish, and at peace ... grow[ing] in the grace and knowledge of our Lord and Savior"* (2 Peter 3:14, 18)? What changes need to occur for this to be true of you? His resurrection power is available to accomplish all that needs to happen.

The Promise of the Lord's Return
2 Peter 3

Issues in 2 Peter

The early church had to deal with false teachers. Those loyal to Judaism argued for a return to a legal requirement for salvation as opposed to salvation by faith. Others, known today as *docetists*, taught that Jesus had not been fully human, denying the essential doctrine of the Incarnation. The greatest threat to orthodox teaching came from Gnosticism, which taught a scheme of salvation based on special knowledge and escape from the material world's corruption. Some of these views are evident in the descriptions of false teachers in 2 Peter 2 and Jude.

Impending Judgment and Concluding Exhortation

Peter opens the last section of his letter by addressing the recipients as *"beloved"*; he refers to it as *"the second letter that I am writing to you"*; and he says both letters were written to *"stir... up your sincere mind"* (3:1). In contrast to the *"blots and blemishes"* (2:13) of false teachers, a *"sincere mind"* is able to withstand heresy. Doctrinal and spiritual purity is maintained by clear and consistent explanation of the Scriptures.

Peter addresses a new error in thinking in 3:3-4. False teachers were scoffing, *"Where is the promise of His coming? For ever since the fathers fell asleep, all things are continuing as they were from the beginning of creation."* At root is the apparent tension between faith in God's promises and the hard realities of worldly existence. Those living in unbelief make wrong *choices* because they make wrong suppositions. *"They deliberately overlook ... the word of God"* (3:5).

Not only are the Creator's characteristics abundantly apparent within His creation, but there has been at least one startling sign of its eventual judgment. In Noah's time, the world was destroyed by water. Even now,

"By the same word the heavens and earth that now exist are stored up for fire, being kept until the day of judgment and destruction of the ungodly" (3:7). The God who created the world can—and some-times does—intervene in it. From time to time, God has brought about unexpected events in history through His Word and His people.

Peter's answer to the taunt of verse 4 is to maintain that with the Lord *"one day is as a thousand years, and a thousand years as one day"* (3:8). Humans may reckon that a delay in the Lord's return is proof that it will never happen, but in God's perspective, 1,000 years is no more than a single day. *"The Lord is not slow to fulfill His promise.... [He] is patient toward you, not wishing that any should perish, but that all should reach repentance"* (3:9). What the false teachers deride as evidence of ineffectualness on God's part is actually evidence of His steadfast mercy.

Christ will return when least expected, and His return will shake the entire cosmos: *"The day of the Lord will come like a thief, and then the heavens will pass away with a roar, and the heavenly bodies will be burned up and dissolved, and the earth and the works that are done on it will be exposed"* (3:10). Everything that humanity regards as permanent, fixed, and eternal, everything that witnesses to humanity's power and pride, will collapse at *"the day of the Lord."*

What will remain after such destruction? God may be trusted not to destroy those for whom His beloved Son died. Therefore, believers ought to prepare themselves for the world to come by living *"lives of holiness and godliness"* (3:11). *"The day of God, ... [when] the heavens will be set on fire and dissolved"* (3:12), Peter repeats. Believers are to wait for and *"hasten... the coming of the day of God,"* not because they glory in destruction, but because they know this is the way to the fulfillment of God's promise. They anticipate *"new heavens and a new earth in which righteousness dwells"* (3:13). Ultimately a time and a realm will come in which righteousness alone will dwell, separated forever from everything contrary to God's holy purpose.

Think about the *"day of the Lord"* (3:10). If it were to come now, would you be ready? Are you keeping close accounts with God? It's a matter of a moment-by-moment walk by faith with Him. Take time to meditate on God's Word in Hebrews 10:35-39. The righteous ones who live by faith are those who are truly ready for the unfolding purposes of God.

Peter may have been influenced by the Judaic belief that the Messiah would come when all Israel kept the Torah perfectly for one day. If 2 Peter 3:12 links the Messiah's coming to the saints' obedience (hastening or speeding its coming), then the Holy Spirit, who guided and guarded Peter's words, wanted the readers to make that connection. However, the more likely meaning, as the nearly identical wording of 3:14 indicates, is that *"be[ing] diligent to be found by Him without spot or blemish, and at peace"* prepares believers to look forward to the Lord's coming instead of fearing or evading it.

Paul's letters contain *"some things ... that are hard to understand, which the ignorant and unstable twist"* (3:16), Peter says. But people also distort *"the other Scriptures"*—and *"to their own destruction."* We have no explanation of exactly how the false teachers misuse Paul's writings. The present reference appears in a section dealing with the delay of Christ's return, and Peter may have been thinking of false interpretations of Paul's teaching on that subject. The Scriptures are the foundation of a proper knowledge of God and a bulwark against false teaching. They can, of course, be misused, as Paul's letters have been in this instance. Their misuse simply results in the *"destruction"* of *"lawless people" "carried away with the error"* (3:17). But rightly understood, the Scriptures are a *"guard"* and a *"secure position."* They promote growth in *"the grace and knowledge of our Lord and Savior Jesus Christ"*—an increase in the knowledge of Christ that overflows to His *"glory both now and to the day of eternity. Amen."* (3:18).

Personalize this lesson.

Repeatedly throughout his letters, Peter warns readers to be aware of error in spiritual matters—both doctrine and lifestyle. Such discernment is based on knowing God's Word, the standard by which we measure all things. Regular study of His Word equips us to discern God's truth and teaches us how to grow into the kind of people God created us to be. Will you ask God to help you develop the commitment you'll need to be consistent about your Bible study?

Facing life's trials is difficult—and inevitable. And sometimes we need more than our own studies. We are better equipped to face trials as members of a faith community—we need to support one another. If you haven't attended a Bible-believing church in a while, will you make it a point to do so this week? If you do attend regularly, will you pray for and support others who might be enduring trials—and be willing to share with others so that they might support you through your trials?

Small Group Leader's Guide

While *Engaging God's Word* is great for personal study, it is generally even more effective and enjoyable when studied with others. Studying with others provides different perspectives and insights, care, prayer support, and fellowship that studying on your own does not. Depending on your personal circumstances, consider studying with your family or spouse, with a friend, in a Sunday school, with a small group at church, work, or in your neighborhood, or in a mentoring relationship.

In a traditional Community Bible Study class, your study would involve a proven four-step method: personal study, a small group discussion facilitated by a trained leader, a lecture covering the passage of Scripture, and a written commentary about the same passage. *Engaging God's Word* provides two of these four steps with the study questions and commentary. When you study with a group, you add another of these—the group discussion. And if you enjoy teaching, you could even provide a modified form of the fourth, the lecture, which in a small group setting might be better termed a wrap-up talk.

Here are some suggestions to help leaders facilitate a successful group study.

1. Decide how long you would like each group meeting to last. For a very basic study, without teaching, time for fellowship, or group prayer, plan on one hour. If you want to allow for fellowship before the meeting starts, add at least 15 minutes. If you plan to give a short teaching, add 15 or 20 minutes. If you also want time for group prayer, add another 10 or 15 minutes. Depending on the components you include for your group, each session will generally last between one and two hours.

2. Set a regular time and place to meet. Meeting in a church classroom or a conference room at work is fine. Meeting in a home is also a good option, and sometimes more relaxed and comfortable.

3. Publicize the study and/or personally invite people to join you.

4. Begin praying for those who have committed to come. Continue to pray for them individually throughout the course of the study.

5. Make sure everyone has his or her own book at least a week before you meet for the first time.

6. Encourage group members to read the first lesson and do the questions before they come to the group meeting.

7. Prepare your own lesson.

8. Prepare your wrap-up talk, if you plan to give one. Here is a simple process for developing a wrap-up talk:

    a. Divide the passage you are studying into two or three divisions. Jot down the verses for each division and describe the content of each with one complete sentence that answers the question, "What is the passage about?"

    b. Decide on the central idea of your wrap-up talk. The central idea is the life-changing principle found in the passage that you believe God wants to implant in the hearts and minds of your group. The central idea answers the question, "What does God want us to learn from this passage?"

    c. Provide one illustration that would make your central idea clear and meaningful to your group. This could be an illustration from your own life, or a story you've read or heard somewhere else.

    d. Suggest one application that would help your group put the central idea into practice.

    e. Choose an aim for your wrap-up talk. The aim answers the question, "What does God want us to do about it?" It encourages specific change in your group's lives, if they choose to respond to the central idea of the passage. Often it takes the form of a question you will ask your group: "Will you, will I choose to … ?"

9. Show up early to the study so you can arrange the room, set up the refreshments (if you are serving any), and welcome people as they arrive.

10. Whether your meeting includes a fellowship time or not, begin the discussion time promptly each week. People appreciate it when you respect their time. Transition into the discussion with prayer, inviting God to guide the discussion time and minister personally to each person present.

11. Model enthusiasm to the group. Let them know how excited you are about what you are learning—and your eagerness to hear what God is teaching them.

12. As you lead through the questions, encourage everyone to participate, but don't force anyone. If one or two people tend to dominate the discussion, encourage quieter ones to participate by saying something like, "Let's hear from someone who hasn't shared yet." Resist the urge to teach during discussion time. This time is for your group to share what they have been discovering.

13. Try to allow time after the questions have been discussed to talk about the "Apply what you have learned," "Think about" and "Personalize this lesson" sections. Encourage your group members in their efforts to partner with God in allowing Him to transform their lives.

14. Transition into the wrap-up talk, if you are doing one (see number 8).

15. Close in prayer. If you have structured your group to allow time for prayer, invite group members to pray for themselves and one another, especially focusing on the areas of growth they would like to see in their lives as a result of their study. If you have not allowed time for group prayer, you as leader can close this time.

16. Before your group finishes their final lesson, start praying and planning for what your next *Engaging God's Word* study will be.

About Community Bible Study

For almost 40 years Community Bible Study has taught the Word of God through in-depth, community-based Bible studies. With nearly 700 classes in the United States as well as classes in more than 70 countries, Community Bible Study purposes to be an "every-person's Bible study, available to all."

Classes for men, women, youth, children, and even babies, are all designed to make members feel loved, cared for, and accepted— regardless of age, ethnicity, socio-economic status, education, or church membership. Because Bible study is most effective in one's heart language, Community Bible Study curriculum has been translated into more than 50 languages.

Community Bible Study makes every effort to stand in the center of the mainstream of historic Christianity, concentrating on the essentials of the Christian faith rather than denominational distinctives. Community Bible Study respects different theological views, preferring to focus on helping people to know God through His Word, grow deeper in their relationships with Jesus, and be transformed into His likeness.

Community Bible Study's focus ... is to glorify God by providing in-depth Bible studies and curriculum in a Christ-centered, grace-filled, and philosophically safe environment.

Community Bible Study's passion ... is the transformation of individuals, families, communities, and generations through the power of God's Word, making disciples of the Lord Jesus Christ.

Community Bible Study's relationship with local churches ... is one of support and respect. Community Bible Study classes are composed of people from many different churches; they are designed to complement and not compete with the ministry of the local church. Recognizing that the Lord has chosen the local church as His primary channel of ministry, Community Bible Study encourages class members to belong to and actively support their local churches and to be servants and leaders in their congregations.

Do you want to experience lasting transformation in your life? Are you ready to go deeper in God's Word? There is probably a Community Bible Study near you! Find out by visiting www.findmyclass.org or scan the QR code on this page.

For more information:

Call   800-826-4181

Email   info@communitybiblestudy.org

Web   www.communitybiblestudy.org

Class   www.findmyclass.org

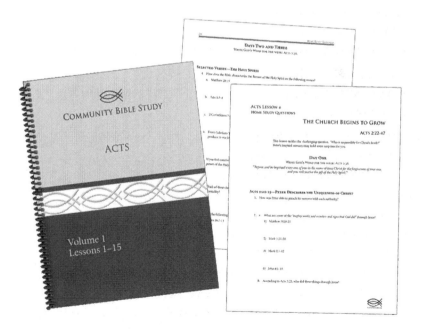

Where will your next Bible study adventure take you?

Engage Bible Studies help you discover the joy and the richness of God's Word and apply it to your life.

Check out these titles for your next adventure:

Engaging God's Word: Genesis

Engaging God's Word: Deuteronomy

Engaging God's Word: Joshua & Judges

Engaging God's Word: Ruth & Esther

Engaging God's Word: Daniel

Engaging God's Word: Job

Engaging God's Word: Mark

Engaging God's Word: Luke

Engaging God's Word: Acts

Engaging God's Word: Romans

Engaging God's Word: Galatians

Engaging God's Word: Ephesians

Engaging God's Word: Philippians

Engaging God's Word: Colossians

Engaging God's Word: 1 & 2 Thessalonians

Engaging God's Word: Hebrews

Engaging God's Word: James

Engaging God's Word: Revelation

Available at Amazon.com and in fine bookstores.

Visit engagebiblestudies.com

Made in the USA
Lexington, KY
29 February 2016